Preparing For Marriage

What To Do Before (And After) You Say "I Do"

Before and After the Wedding: An interactive guide and online resource assisting you on your journey from Dating until "Death Do Us Part"

Workbook, Audio, and Video Files

Written and facilitated by
Jim Adams III, *Certified Marriage Intensive Coach*, and
Teresa Adams, *MAMFT, LPC, NCC*

© 2015 by Family Matters First, LLC
All Rights Reserved

No part of this publication may be reproduced, stored in a retrieval system, or transmitted in any form or by any means, without the prior permission of the author or publisher, except for brief quotations in articles or reviews.

THE HOLY BIBLE, NEW INTERNATIONAL VERSION®, NIV® Copyright © 1973, 1978, 1984, 2011 by Biblica, Inc.® Used by permission. All rights reserved worldwide.

Scripture taken from the NEW AMERICAN STANDARD BIBLE®, Copyright © 1960, 1962, 1963, 1968, 1971, 1972, 1973, 1975, 1977, 1995 by The Lockman Foundation. Used by permission.

Scripture quotations are taken from the Holy Bible, New Living Translation, copyright ©1996, 2004, 2007 by Tyndale House Foundation. Used by permission of Tyndale House Publishers, Inc., Carol Stream, Illinois 60188. All rights reserved.

The King James Version of the Bible is in the public domain.

Printed in the United States of America

ISBN 13: 978-0692378625
ISBN 10: 0692378626

Couples' Workbook
Table of Contents

Get the Most Out of "Preparing for Marriage"	5
Introduction	7
Preface	13
Session 1: Do Marriage Right	17
Session 2: So You Want to Get Married?	23
Session 3: Great Expectations	35
Session 4: Lose Your Mind If You Want to Love Your Spouse	49
Session 5: Do You Know What You Are About To Do? Covenant or Contract?	61
Session 6: Communicate or Your Marriage Will Disintegrate	75
Session 7: Caring Enough to Embrace Conflict	91
Session 8: Roles and Responsibilities: Being a Godly Husband and a Godly Wife	109
Session 9: The Money	129
Session 10: Sanctified, Satisfying, and Sizzling Married Sex!	135
Session 11: Prepared Parents	151
Session 12: The Blended/Bonded Family: "We Do…Again"	171
Session 13: Making Godly Decisions: Are You Sure You Want To Do This?	181
Acknowledgments	199
About the Authors	201

Church/Civic Groups	207
Notes	209
Testimonials	215

Get the Most Out of "Preparing for Marriage"

Our goal with this book is to provide the single greatest resource to help you on your journey toward the most amazing marriage possible.

To help make this book exactly that, we have included much more than just the book.

There is accompanying audio and video for each chapter that you can access – for FREE – that will help instill some of these lessons permanently into your life.

To download the free audio and access all of the other resources, please visit:
www.RelationshipSuccessUniversity.com/bookguide

Introduction

Some decades ago, a popular bumper sticker sported a quote that read, "When All Else Fails, Read the Instructions," superimposed over the outline of a Bible. The implication was that when you have tried everything, and everything has failed, try JESUS.

Now we aren't against trying Jesus. As a matter of fact, Teresa and I both "tried Jesus" before we were teens and we love Him, maybe because He first loved us. But that bumper sticker always made me think, *Why don't we read the instructions before everything else fails?*

Most would agree that the institution of marriage is under siege, and many marriages are failing, but don't despair. We have a cure, a success strategy, and here it is: Why not understand exactly what you are about to do, before you do it? God invented marriage according to Genesis 2:18-24, and He left an instruction manual.

This book – well, actually it's more of a supplemental resource to an online seminar – is a collection of

> "Which sounds more romantic? Is it more romantic to say, 'Beloved, I see that the divorce rate is 50%. Let's get married anyway and let's assume that our love is so special, so passionate, so superior to all those other couples, that we'll make it – that we'll stay together till death us do part.' Or, can we get to the place where people will realize that the true romantic would say, 'Beloved, the divorce rate is 50%. I want to marry you and I love you so much that I want to learn everything the experts know about what makes marriage succeed or fail so that we can work to make sure our love and our marriage last, til death us do part.'
>
> I believe that in the near future – if those of us in the coalition do our job – couples will come to accept that the most romantic thing they can do is to walk hand-in-hand into a course on making marriages work. That taking such a course will become as much a part of the wedding tradition as the bridal shower or the bachelor party. That **not** taking such a course will come to be seen as foolhardy, reckless, uninformed, and unsophisticated. That the time will come when none of us would dream of giving our children a big wedding and not also giving them a marriage education class. That we will also know what to give them at the first baby shower. That along with prenatal classes a couple will also sign up for a booster course on keeping love alive. And that employers and insurers will come to recognize that such courses will easily pay for themselves."
>
> —Diane Sollee
> Director of Smart Marriages

our personal stories, struggles, and successes in our 30-year marriage journey, coupled with thousands of hours as professional counselors and a marriage success plan that we believe is inspired by Almighty God. This resource is your instruction manual based on God's original design and plan. In it, you will find written instructions and links to audios and videos.

If you follow these instructions, the slaughterhouse of marriage failure will not be your destiny. Instead, you marriage will be happy, holy, and heavenly. The instruction manual declares it to be so!
This manual is designed to help you prepare for a God-honoring relationship in marriage; a marriage that will last; and a marriage that will be healthy, holy, and happy. After all, God invented marriage, according to Genesis 2:18, and God performed the first marriage ceremony, according to Genesis 2:22. Marriage as an institution and individual marriages fail when we deviate from the plan and the foundation set by Almighty God.

How to best use this manual:

1. **Self-directed premarital study and preparation.** Be very intentional. You and your spouse-to-be should sit down and thoroughly go through this manual. Do the assignments together. Compare your answers. Be honest with each other.

2. **With a licensed marriage counselor or coach.** Make this study manual the basis for individual counseling sessions. Prepare for each session by studying and discussing the manual, while a spiritually mature couple or marriage professional serves as your guide/marriage mentor.

3. **Group sessions.** Make this study manual the basis for group counseling sessions. You and your spouse-to-be along with a number of other couples seriously considering marriage will prepare for each session by studying and discussing the manual, while a spiritually mature couple or marriage professional will serve as your guide/marriage mentor.

4. **Weekend intensives.** A trained marriage professional, experienced and spiritually mature couple, or marriage mentor will lead you and your spouse-to-be or your small group of couples for a weekend intensive. Weekend intensives are Friday evenings from 5:00 p.m. to 8:00 p.m. and Saturdays from 8:30 a.m. to 5:30 p.m. This is the equivalent of 10 to 12 weekly sessions combined into one weekend.

5. **Church-wide or community-wide seminars.** Invite Jim and Teresa into your church or community to personally lead and conduct a seminar. Seminars typically start Friday evening and continue all day Saturday.

Now, you might be asking yourself, "What if I am already married?" As the ancient proverb goes,

"For a man who is traveling down the wrong road, it is never too late to turn around." So even if you are already married, this study offers an opportunity to "go back to the basics, and get a fresh start."

You will find this tool full of useful information even if you have been married for many, many, years.

Our Approach

Our approach to successful preparation involves:

- Modern technology – online couples' assessment tools
- Our own experiences – twenty-nine years of marriage, combined with the marriage experiences of your facilitators
- Professional training – a Master's level marriage and family therapist
- Workbooks – to use as a reference during your marriage
- Biblically based truths – our foundation is the instruction book written by the very Inventor of marriage

Remember, not every couple who has gone through this manual has decided to get married, and many others have postponed their marriages.

This is a Good Thing!

The first time we used this manual in a weekend intensive, we met with a young couple Friday evening from 5:30 p.m. to 9:00 p.m., started again Saturday morning at 9:00 a.m., and broke for lunch at noon. The couple had an assignment to complete during lunch. At 1:00 p.m. we received a call informing us that while they were doing their assignment, they came to the conclusion that they should not be married. Teresa and I had seen the warning signs from the very beginning (starting with the assessment). The young man, however, gave his life to Christ during the Saturday morning session.

It is up to us to reveal information that will allow prospective married couples to identify the current and potential issues that may block their path to a healthy and long-lasting marriage, and determine their willingness to overcome those issues. This manual is designed to SAVE marriages, not stop them!

We are constantly amazed at how many couples uncover problems while they're dating, only to ignore them because they are "so in love"...with the idea of being married. Do not ignore the warning signs this manual will help you uncover. Warning signs do not necessarily mean the marriage is not going to work, but ignoring them typically leads to failed marriages.

If we had a dollar for every time we heard a couple say, "I knew he or she was selfish, abusive, overly bonded with his or her mother or father, or (you fill in the blank) while we were dating, but I thought after we were married, things would improve," we would have a lot of dollars.

This manual is designed to "force" couples to think and discuss many of the practical issues most couples do not discuss.

This guidebook will allow you to:

- Assess yourself and begin to understand your fiance or spouse.
- Determine how prepared you are for marriage.
- Help you prepare for marriage.
- Uncover problems and areas of conflict.
- Offer Biblical answers and solutions for dealing with them.

Jim and I are going to make you a promise. Statistically, experts say that couples who undergo premarital counseling have a 75 percent chance of staying married. Taking this a step further, we guarantee that if you diligently devote yourself to studying this manual, doing the exercises, answering the questions, offering an honest assessment, and then DOING what you have learned to do as a result of your training, your marriage has a 100 percent chance of success. There...we said it!

If you are single and want to be married, our advice for you is to pray, wait, communicate, and investigate.

If you have been married before, the most important thing is not to be concerned with the state of your previous marriage(s), but rather to focus on the strength of your commitment to the marriage you are in *today*. You can't change what happened in the past, but you can begin transforming your present marriage into one that honors Christ.

Do you have a real commitment to the "institution" and "covenant" of marriage, or do you have a casual interest in the "idea" of marriage?

Special Bonus Resource

Every chapter or session has an accompanying audio with Jim and Teresa discussing the information included in the chapter. The audio is not a replacement for the manual. While we recognize people have different learning styles (some verbal, some visual, some both) we encourage you to read and work through the manual. The audio allows you to listen via your smart phone, tablet, laptop, desktop, or any internet-enabled device.

The audio file also means you don't have to stop doing something to listen. Listen to the audio while you're working out at the gym, walking, driving, cooking, cleaning, mountain climbing, scuba diving (okay maybe not), but you get the picture. At the end of each chapter, there will be a link to the corresponding audio file.

But Wait! There's More!

In addition to the written word and the spoken word, we also have a collection of videos, the... uh..."videoed" word, available on the Family Matters First YouTube channel.

Access our YouTube videos at http://www.RelationshipSuccessUniversity.com/bookguide. New videos are constantly being added.

This marriage journey is just that – a journey. As you go through this manual, you will receive a marriage head start that sets you up for success. For your continued success, visit http://www.RelationshipSuccessUniversity.com where you will find a library of more than 6,000 videos (think of it as a Netflix of resources) on dating, marriage, parenting, conflict resolution, communication, finances, sexual intimacy, personal spiritual growth, and more.

Preface

Let us ask you a question.

Does it seem strange that couples spend thousands of dollars on the wedding and almost nothing on the marriage? The majority of couples spend between $18,900 and $31,500 on their wedding day. According to www.costofwedding.com, couples in the United States spend an average of $25,200 for their wedding, excluding the cost of a honeymoon or an engagement ring. This data is current as of 2015.

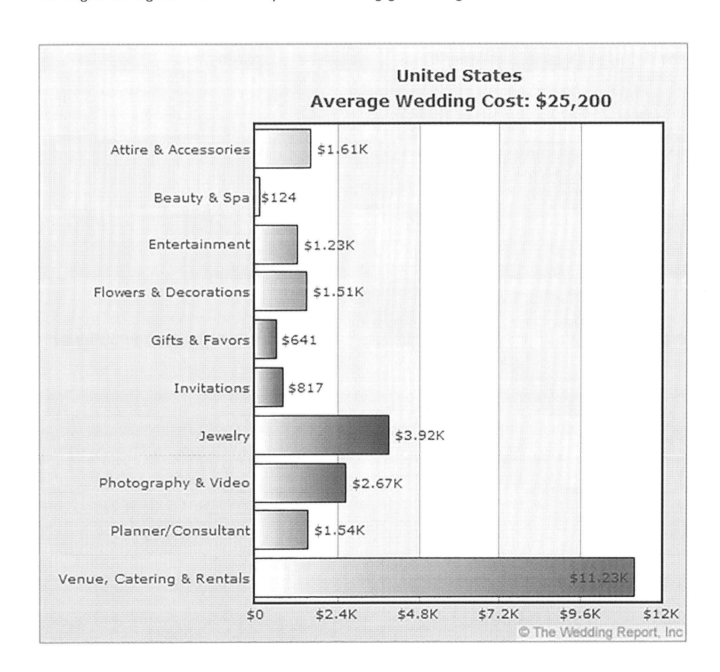

The average engaged couple spends an average of 250 hours on planning their wedding and only two hours planning a successful marriage.

Now according to most sources, the average marriage in the United States only lasts eight years before the couple gets divorced. So, after spending thousands of dollars on your wedding day, and hundreds of hours on your wedding ceremony, wouldn't it make sense to spend at least a few dollars on your marriage? Of course it would. The wedding lasts but a few moments; the marriage is designed to last a lifetime.

Talk about being penny-wise and pound-foolish! No wonder marriages fail. But don't despair. That's why God invented pre-marital counseling. Your marriage doesn't have to be just another poor statistic. Help is available! As a matter of fact, by the grace of Almighty God – the Inventor of marriage – your marriage will not become another poor statistic if you spend time properly preparing, growing, and learning together.

Did you go to high school? Let's say the answer is yes. What about college? Let's say yes again. So you have spent 8 years in school (not including graduate and post-graduate work) preparing yourself to be whatever you were preparing to be. All you know about being married, on the other hand, is what you learned at home (and maybe your parents' marriage wasn't a successful one), on television, or from friends who may not even be married.

We have spent the last 30 years (as of May 2015) in a wonderful marriage, and we have four children. We dated for four years before we were married when we were at age 22. In our efforts to improve our own marriage, we became passionate about improving the marriages of others.

You don't have to be a wicked wife, a horrible husband, a misguided mom, or a drop-out dad. You have come to the right place. We can help!

You will notice as we proceed through this study that the Bible is used frequently as the final authority on issues of life and marriage. The Bible speaks clearly and powerfully on the subject of marriage and on the struggles men and women face. After all, it was Almighty God who created man, then woman from man, and then presented woman to man. Since marriage is God's idea, it makes sense to turn to the Creator for our source of instruction and information.

It is our desire to impart the truth as it relates to God's Word. In that respect, we are like the mail carrier. The Postmaster General has given us a letter to deliver, and we are delivering the mail.

The Gospel was designed to "go" into the world. We are only the messengers, just a delivery service, so please don't shoot us!

May the words of our mouths and the meditation of our hearts be acceptable in the sight of Almighty God.

Session 1: Do Marriage Right

A Dangerous Journey

Several years ago, we took a family trip to Colorado. We rented a condo in Dillon and spent nine days traveling through Vail, Denver and Colorado Springs, and had the opportunity to see the Rocky Mountain National Park and Pike's Peak. The latter is so steep that there is a mandatory stopping point about halfway down the mountainside so that every driver can stop and check their car's brakes. Knowing that the mountainside is so steep, many drivers simply "ride their brakes." This can actually cause the brakes to overheat and ultimately fail. And if the brakes fail, the vehicle will careen down the side of the mountain.

Well, imagine you are at the top of the mountain and strapped in the back seat of your car are your two little children. You and your spouse are about to start down the mountainside when you see it is littered with wrecked cars and broken bodies of people who have tried to make this journey.

This story paints the picture of marriage in America. The road is cluttered with wrecked relationships, and the moms, dads, and children are all victims.

So what do we do?

We have three answers.

1. The main thing we need to do is teach the drivers how to drive. That's why we developed this information. We have a vicious cycle in America: broken homes produce broken people that have more broken homes that produce more broken people. But it's not an irreversible cycle. We need to teach people how to have Godly marriages. Don't you find it odd that more teaching is required to get a driver's license than a marriage license?

    People get married with no preparation, training, or any idea of what marriage means. No wonder marriages are broken.

2. We need to have a heart full of love and compassion for those who have wrecked. We need to

remember that God loves them and does not hold grudges. Many people actually get married with no thought, no idea, and not even the awareness of pre-marital classes.

As a result, they start down the mountain and they wreck.

We spend many hours in the counseling center working to restore these individuals, and from time to time we are able to help put the marriage back together. We have seen divorced couples remarry. The damage done to the children in a divorce often requires years of counseling to correct, but we are compassionate. After all, "You don't know what you don't know."

Unfortunately in marriage, however, what you don't know can "kill" the marriage.

3. We need to construct some guardrails. The devil has leveled all the artillery of hell against our homes. We need to build some guardrails and remove some of the obstacles that are causing the disastrous wrecks.

   Satan does not want to see healthy, happy, and holy marriages. Once you understand that, you will realize the need to take certain precautions. In other words, guard yourself. While we are not called to be isolated from the world, we are called to be insulated from the world. Pre-marital classes are a means of constructing guardrails.

This book is filled with marriage "guardrails" to prevent you from, figuratively speaking, wrecking and killing someone and literally killing your marriage.

The slaughterhouse of relationship failure does not have to be your destiny. We can teach you how to succeed. We promise!

Do Marriage Right

Your mission, should you choose to accept it, is to build a righteous relationship, a mighty marriage, a fantastic family, and become a prepared parent. You will hear and benefit from personal experience, professional training, and practical application.

"Do Marriage Right" has a two-fold meaning:

1. Make sure you are properly trained and prepared to "do" your marriage the correct way. Chances are if you are like most people who get married, you have no idea what the "right way" actually is. Don't despair; that's why we have created this resource, so you can be assured you are ready to do your marriage right.

2. You are about to become part of a proud and sacred institution – traditional, biblical marriage. When a marriage fails, it's not just the individual marriage that fails. Each failed marriage adds fuel to the popular 21st century misconception that marriage has lost its luster. Each failure turns up the volume on the "Why should I get married?" questions.

As part of this sacred institution, we need you to join in the fight with us to help spread the word that marriage is not dead, boring, or a death sentence. It is not doomed to fail. On the contrary, marriage is alive, exciting, and allows two people to really live as one. You can have a successful marriage – guaranteed – if you will follow the directions. Not only will your personal marriage thrive, but you will be part of a growing movement to renew, revitalize, and reinvigorate the very institution of marriage.

Notes

Let's Get Started: Introductions

Allow all couples to introduce themselves. Provide suggested topics so each person is sharing similar information. Here are some ideas:

- "How did you meet?"
- "How long have you been dating?"
- "When are you getting married?"
- "Why do you feel this is the right person for you to marry?"
- "Do you have anything else you want to share?"

Introduction and Preface

After reading the introduction and preface, please share any information you found to be interesting regarding:

- The cost of weddings today
- How little effort goes into marriage preparation

Discuss:

1. Why did you enroll in this class or purchase this workbook?
2. What do you hope to gain from these sessions?
3. How well do you believe you know your spouse-to-be?
4. Are there issues you have noticed while you've been dating that are of concern to either of you?
5. Have you discussed them?
6. Did you realize the Bible has a lot to say about marriage?

Relationship Assessment

We are big believers in the power and insight offered by using assessments. We have personally completed personal assessments, couples assessments, parenting assessments, leadership assessments and assessments to determine spiritual gifts.

We have done more assessments than we can count. When we are personally counseling a couple as part of a weekend intensive, we always start with a relationship assessment, and we recommend you do the same.

We offer a user-friendly online system used to empower people to communicate each other's unique needs, feelings, and expectations in a way that is clear, direct and constructive. This unique tool provides a visual resource that helps improve mutual understanding, clarify relationship dynamics, measure progress and reveal what is needed for greater relationship success.

RSU Couples Assessment is designed to show individuals how they can improve their relationships by gaining insights from themselves and those they interact with. In many cases, learning about yourself from those you interact with can be even more empowering than a self-assessment. It can show you how to further succeed in your relationship(s). Who each of us is a combination of three perspectives: how we see us; how the world sees us; and how we really are. This helps you to really see yourself and view areas for growth as well as areas of potential danger in your relationship.

The RSU assessment generates deep and productive conversations that couples would not otherwise have about their relationship. These conversations restore insight and understanding, revive relationship and renew intimacy.

What does an assessment typically cost? We recommend couples complete two assessments. A personal assessment and a

Notes

couple's assessment. Since this is so important and since we are striving to make this the ONE resource for your relationship success, we offer this to our readers for at no additional cost.

 To register for your free assessment additional resources, go to: www.RelationshipSuccessUniversity.com/bookguide.

Session 2: So You Want to Get Married?

'We are here because it doesn't make sense to spend more time preparing for a driver's license than for a marriage license.'

Marriage Preparation 101

> "The best thing you can do is anticipate problems and try to solve them before they occur. You do this when you go to your doctor for a routine physical exam or when you go to the dentist for your preventative cleaning and checkup. You do this when you take your car in for a tune-up and oil change. Why not try a little marital troubleshooting?
>
> Unfortunately, many young people think marriage will *solve* problems, as if saying "I do" is a magical cure. The opposite is true
>
> Marriage only intensifies existing problems. That is why it is best to identify potential problems ahead of time."
>
> -- Louis McBurney, M.D.

Here are some ways to do that:

Thoroughly Discuss Your Expectations

Each partner carries into marriage a huge bag full of expectations. Men and women assume things will transpire just the way they imagine:

- "We will visit *my* family each Christmas."
- "My husband will be home every evening."
- "My wife will have a hot, four-course meal on the table when I come home."
- "We will never argue or disagree."
- "My wife will love watching football all weekend."
- "My husband will not continue to watch football all weekend."

More than likely, your expectations were formed by what you observed in your home while you were growing up. Remember, though, your spouse's family may have been much different than your own. Just because your dad helped wash the dishes, that doesn't mean your husband will do that for you. If your mother kept an immaculate house, don't automatically assume your wife will be as committed to cleanliness.

If your expectations differ, conflict will result. The more you discuss your expectations ahead of time, the better your chances of blending together happily.

Learn to Resolve Conflicts

Many young couples believe a happy marriage has no conflict. Not so! Disagreements, hassles, and conflicts are inevitable. Happily married couples are those who have learned to resolve conflict through communication, negotiation, compromise, and sacrifice.

Conflicts must be resolved for a relationship to survive. Burying your hurts and struggles is like carrying around a sack of rocks. Every new hurt you bury becomes another rock you drag around. Eventually, the load becomes too heavy and the relationship falls apart.

Resolving conflict is hard work. I'm the kind of person who's comfortable when everybody's happy. For me, it's only the commitment to my mate that keeps me working. I've learned, for the sake of my marriage, I have to face conflicts, not run from them.

Go See Your Doctor

Most states require a premarital blood test, which detects certain diseases. Even if your state doesn't require one, it is still wise to get tested if either you or your spouse-to-be has been sexually active. If a sexually transmitted disease does exist, your doctor will explain the ramifications and treatment.

Your physician can also discuss birth control options if you plan to delay having children.

Get Premarital Counseling

A lot of people are afraid of counseling because they think it means they're sick or have something terribly wrong with them. But many people seek a counselor to help avoid problems. This is especially important for marriage. A trained expert can point out problems that may arise and guide you toward resolutions.

1. Watch the Family Matters First YouTube Series, "12 Must-Ask Questions Before You Get Married"

    http://www.RelationshipSuccessUniversity.com/bookguide

2. Review each of your credit reports together as a couple

Notes

We will review this step in greater detail in the session titled, "The Money," but we highly recommend you do this prior to marriage. This is not only a great (and honest) way to reveal your financial histories to each other, but it is also a great way to take a careful and calculated look at your own personal credit history – something many neglect. You can receive a copy of your credit report FREE once a year at https://www.annualcreditreport.com.

Session 2: So You Want to Get Married?

Questions:

List 7 reasons you want to marry this person:

1. _____

_____

2. _____

_____

3. _____

_____

4. _____

_____

5. _____

_____

6. _____

_____

7. _____

_____

How do you know this is the person you are to marry?

_____

_____

How did you decide this is the person you want to marry?

_____

_____

Are you aware of the biblical mandate concerning who to marry in 2 Corinthians 6:14-18?

____ Yes ____ No

What does this mean?

_____

_____

Affirm that your fiancé is also aware of this biblical mandate. ____ Yes ____ No

Does your intended spouse meet these qualifications?

____ Yes ____ No

How is your vision and your hearing? Before you answer, think about the question. Everyone sees and hears through the lenses of past experiences. We all bring baggage into a relationship and that baggage affects what we see, think, and hear.

_____

_____

Real-Life Example: During the early part of our marriage, Teresa was a stay-at-home mom. Even though this idea is lost in most marriages today, I was certain it was God's plan for our family at the time, so I discussed this plan with her even while we were dating.

We had a shared checking account and I was the bookkeeper (family finances are discussed in a later chapter). I had no problem giving Teresa money when she asked for it, but one day she said to me in an exasperated voice, "You know, coming to you and asking for money reminds me of when I had to go ask my daddy for money. It makes me feel like a little girl."

Her perception was based on the baggage she carried from past experiences. Even though I was not treating her like a little girl she felt like one, based on her history. Does this make sense? The moral of the story is that our histories have clouded our vision and hearing and the clearer we understand that the better (and clearer) we will hear and see.

Most people have no idea how much their past influences them or even that it does influence them to begin with. Everybody has a history, a story, and baggage from their past. The important thing to understand is how your story affects who you are now and why you do the things you do today.

For better or worse, we are all significantly shaped by the kinds of family lives we've experienced. But while we are products of the past, we are not prisoners of the past…unless we choose to be.

We'd better understand who we are by understanding where we come from. So let's examine the similarities and differences between where you and your dating partner or potential spouse come from.

Discuss:

- Your parents' marriage (whether they are divorced; separated; together; or had a good, poor, or fair marriage)
- The family rules you had growing up
- How your family handled problems
- Your family beliefs and values
- Your family views on finances
- Your views about the roles and responsibilities of the husband/father and wife/mother
- Your views about work, recreation, and hobbies

We all leave our parents' home with assets and baggage. Unfortunately, what was observed at the home is often repeated in a new relationship.

Obviously some of the things we observed are healthy (assets) and some are not (baggage or liabilities). While our past does not have to become a hitching post (meaning we are stuck there) and it can become a guidepost (meaning we learn and improve). We have to be very cautious and very intentional that our past does not continue to haunt and negatively impact our present and future.

Some examples of what you may or may not have seen in the home you grew up in. Mark each as an asset and liability.

My parents were able to disagree without being disagreeable _____ Yes _____ No

Disagreements typically turned into verbal assaults and insults _____ Yes _____ No

My parents were committed and understood the permanence of marriage _____ Yes _____ No

My parents didn't believe in being very affectionate _____ Yes _____ No

We had family meals together _____ Yes _____ No

We very seldom had family meals together _____ Yes _____ No

My parents taught me the value of hard work and responsibility _____ Yes _____ No

My father/mother was an alcoholic _____ Yes _____ No

My parents were affectionate to each other and to the children _____ Yes _____ No

God was a big part of our family life _____ Yes _____ No

We went to church a lot _____ Yes _____ No

We had regular family devotions _____ Yes _____ No

What about your in-laws?

- Do they support this marriage?
- What are some common mistakes you see in-laws make?
- How could you work to improve in-law relationships?

Does your prospective mate seem to have issues with any of the following?

- Was your prospective mate overly bonded with his or her mother or father?
- Did your prospective mate allow his or her mother or father to dominate your relationship?
- Does your prospective mate take his or her parents' side against you?
- Does your prospective mate compares you to his or her parents?
- Does your prospective mate put the wishes of his or her parents about yours?

Notes

1. Read Genesis 2:24. How should this verse play out in a marriage?

2. Which personal assets would you need to leave home with?

3. What are some of your personal goals? How do those personal goals fit into a marriage?

4. If you could change one thing about your upbringing, what would it be?

Session 2: So You Want to Get Married?

Satan hides in the shadows of our strengths." In Jim"s case, for example, the fact that he has a "laser like focus" can be a strength. It allows him to set a goal and work toward that goal no matter what. It's the kind of focus that allowed him to finish a football game in college after tearing his MCL in the second quarter, but it can also be a liability. He can be so focused on what he wants to accomplish and what he wants done that he can forget to be sensitive to others and maybe even to the voice of God.

5. How does this expression play out in your life?

_____

_____

_____

6. I believe every man and woman needs the following men in his or her life: a great dad, a strong male mentor, and Jesus. How many did you have or do you have?

_____

7. If you did not have either of the first two (and even if you did), do you understand why the third man is so important?

_____ Yes _____ No

Session 3: Great Expectations

Expectations about marriage have a huge impact on a person's level of satisfaction with his or her marriage. To a large degree, the happiness or disappointment you will experience in your marriage will be based on how your marriage experiences match what you thought they would be. Unfortunately, many people base their expectations on false assumptions about what they believe a marriage should be, rather than reality.

Below are some common expectations and fantasies people have about marriage. Circle the ones you agree with and let's discuss them.

1. There will be no real conflict in our marriage.
2. Love is all we need for a good marriage.
3. Our marriage will be a lot like my parents' marriage.
4. Some things are just understood, and if I have to verbalize them, it means my spouse is not paying attention.
5. My spouse and I are on the same page about sex.
6. My spouse knows what really makes me happy.
7. I believe I really know my spouse.
8. My spouse will meet all my relationship and companionship needs.
9. Having a child will improve our relationship.
10. Certain household responsibilities are for men and others are for women.

> "Can two people walk together without agreeing on the direction."
>
> -- Amos 3:3

Read Proverbs 13:12:

1. How does your belief about any of the previous statements match your partner's beliefs about them?

___

2. List some personal expectations you have from your mate.

___

3. Why is it important to know specifically what each of you expects from one another?

___

4. What do you think your spouse expects of you in marriage?

___

You can <u>deal</u> with the unmet expectations and grow your marriage at the same time.

Session 3: Great Expectations

Four Great Ways to Deal with Unmet Expectations in Marriage

1. Love and forgive your spouse. When you exchange marriage vows, you commit before God and your spouse that you will stay committed through everything. Honor this commitment, in spite of your spouse's failures, and the fact that he or she falls short of your expectations.

    The need for forgiveness will never go away in your marriage, so become good at it!

2. Communicate with the intent of understanding your spouse. Many expectations go unmet in our marriages because spouses are not <u>aware of what each expected</u>. The only way to know what each of you expects is to talk about it. Make regular <u>communication</u> part of your marriage.

    Don't make knowing your spouse's expectations a guessing game…talk about them.

3. Change your perspective. In the real world of marriage, you will never be able to meet all of your spouse's needs and he or she will never be able to meet all of yours. We were never intended to do so.

    Some needs can only be met by God alone. Develop this perspective and allow your spouse grace in some areas.

4. Don't throw your expectations out the window. Just because some expectations may be unrealistic and unfair to your spouse, that doesn't mean you need to lose hope in them or your spouse.

Part of the purpose of your marriage is to help one another grow.

> "<u>Continue</u> to strive toward your hopes and aspirations. Work toward them, <u>pray about</u> them, and do it all together."
>
> -- Jackie Bledsoe, Jr.

Notes

To listen to the podcast with Jackie and Stephana Bledsoe, plus additional resources, go to www.RelationshipSuccessUniversity.com/bookguide

Bob Baker, the director of the *Colorado Marriage Projects,* says in *Expectations in Marriage:*

When people enter into the marriage relationship, they bring with them a large, multi-faceted assortment of hopes and dreams that come from multiple life experiences. These hopes and dreams are what we commonly call expectations—a set of beliefs about the way things will be or should be in life. Expectations include such things as roles, life and death issues, relationship models, human behavior, romance, right and wrong, smart vs. stupid, responsibility, consequences for conduct, etc. The Bible speaks to the bottom-line issues associated with unmet expectations in Proverbs 13:12: "Hope deferred makes the heart sick, but a longing fulfilled is a tree of life."

One of the keys to a healthy marriage is the development of a strategy (custom made for every couple) for understanding, communicating, and analyzing the assortment of expectations that each person brings into the relationship. For example, as a couple prepares for marriage, they need to examine the simple question of "What does the husband do when he is not at work?" (and vice-versa for the wife). My wife grew up in a home where Mom stayed at home and Dad worked 8 to 5 for the federal government.

For most of his career, her dad was home on Saturday mornings working in the yard, fixing up the house, painting projects, grooming and training the dog, cleaning out the garage, and washing the family car. When we got married, my wife was probably surprised that I did not do the same things on Saturday mornings. We had an opportunity to discuss "expectations." It is critically important to a marriage to deal directly with expectations.

If ignored or left unattended, unmet expectations inevitably lead to deep feelings of sadness, disappointment, hurt, hopelessness, frustration, and anger (a "sick heart" in the

Session 3: Great Expectations

scripture quoted previously). In general, people feel either content or disappointed with life in direct proportion to how well their life matches what they expected. So, what exactly are we talking about in marriage?

Here are some additional expectations that people bring into marriage:

- We will always feel in love.
- We will keep the same level of commitment we had at the beginning.
- We will basically make each other happy.
- Our romance and sex life will remain fresh and exciting.
- We will share the same goals and interests.
- We will be in agreement on issues of morality, honesty, justice, etc.
- We won't have any serious fights or conflicts without resolution.
- We will share a set of common friends.
- We will be supportive of each other's interests, careers, and other demands outside the home.

Discuss how the "influencers" below affect our expectations for better or for worse:

- Parents and family
- Television and music
- Past relationships
- Friends
- Religious traditions and beliefs
- Cultural background
- Personality differences

What are some of the relational traps associated with expectations? The authors of *Fighting for Your Marriage*, an excellent book on many marital topics by Dr. Scott Stanley and others, report these common hang-ups associated with expectations.

We are often somewhat unaware of our own expectations...they may be present, but only subconsciously. They may be unreasonable. They may have never been voiced.

Your spouse may be unwilling to work toward meeting our expectations, even those that are reasonable. Sometimes expectations are packaged in "I want you to change" messages designed to transform you into the person your spouse expected you to be.

Over a 45-year marriage, Carol and I have been confronted with God's Word on this subject many times. First, God tells us that it is He who wants to map out plans for us:

"I know the plans I have for you, plans to prosper you and not to harm you, plans to give you hope and a future." And he then speaks to our man-made plans (including the ones we have for our mate) with these words:

- Psalm 146:9: "The Lord...frustrates the plans of the wicked."
- Proverbs 16:9: "We can make our plans, but the Lord determines our steps."
- Proverbs 21:30: "Human plans, no matter how wise or well advised, cannot stand against the Lord."

The bottom line seems to be this:

Expectations are worth working through with your mate because "a longing fulfilled is a tree of life" (Proverbs 13:12), and we should make sure any plans that we have for our mate are the same as those planned by God. Otherwise, we are on the losing side of the equation.

May the Lord give you grace and wisdom as you discover and strategize with your spouse about your respective expectations.

 Listen to our interview with Bob Baker, regarding expectations in marriage on www.RelationshipSuccessUniversity.com/bookguide.

Session 3: Great Expectations

Closely related to the problem of unmet and unrealistic expectations in a marriage is the problem of the fairytale marriage. Let's talk about that issue:

Having a Fairytale Marriage Without the Fairytale

And they lived happily ever after….

While people do live happily ever after, many other parts are just a fairytale.

Let's take a few moments to discuss the fairytales you may have heard and let's look at the truth:

Fairytale: Marriage is a 50/50 proposition.

Truth: Marriage is actually about each person doing and giving 100% no matter what the other person is doing or giving. Marriage is not "I will meet you halfway." Marriage is not "If you do this, I will do that."

While it is easier for me to be loving and giving if my spouse is loving and giving, my responsibility is to be loving and giving no matter how my spouse may actually be at any given moment.

Fairytale: "It is a good idea to live together before we get married, so we can try this relationship out."

Truth: This is so *wrong* I don't know where to start. I know. Let's start with what the Creator of marriage says in, I Corinthians 7:2; "Nevertheless, to avoid fornication, let every man have his own wife and let every woman have her own husband."

Fornication is defined as illicit intimate sex between a man and woman who are not currently married. So, the original reason not to live together is that when God designed marriage, He said not to do it. Actually no other reasons are needed, but I realize that today's liberated couples may want additional information.

Research shows that cohabitating before marriage leads to greater chances of divorce. Living together without any commitment (other than to "try it out") leads to an unhealthy pattern of coming and going as you please. This may happen, for example, if you leave over a disagreement and spend the night with a parent or friend to temporarily separate yourself from your spouse for a cooling-off period.

This is not a healthy pattern to continue should you get married. Even when you have the "piece of paper" that says you're married (and by the way, marriage is so much more than a piece of paper) the unhealthy pattern of leaving and coming home has already been established, and it will continue in your marriage.

I can't tell you how many couples come to one of our counseling sessions, some of which are in local churches, and sign up for Christian premarital counseling while they're living together. Most couples are so influenced by today's culture, even though they may not realize it, they have suppressed or completely ignored the fact that this is biblically unacceptable. Don't even start with the arguments that it makes financial sense, etc. What if you are already living together? An ancient proverb says, "For the man traveling down the wrong road headed in the wrong direction, it is never too late to turn around."

What does this statement mean to you?

_____

_____

_____

Session 3: Great Expectations

Living together prior to marriage sets a pattern of non-commitment that continues through the marriage.

Fairytale: I plan to stay married as long as I stay in love.

Truth: Marriage is a covenant commitment that you are making before Almighty God and has nothing to do with your feelings. When a man and a woman decide to get married, it is certainly because they have romantic feelings for each other, but the decision to stay married has more to do with the covenant you made than how you might feel at any given moment. Emotions come and go, but a covenant is forever.

It's important to be very intentional and proactive to make sure the feelings you have for one another grow stronger and stronger, but ultimately "I no longer love him or her" is not an acceptable reason to end a marriage. A couple stays married because of their commitment to Almighty God, the institution of marriage, and to each other more than because of any romantic emotion.

Fairytale: My parents, in-laws, and friends, as well as the people I see on TV, have a perfect marriage and my marriage seems to be hard and not so perfect.

Truth: Every marriage has conflict. You might be thinking, *Wait a minute, Jim, I never saw my parents argue.* I will let you in on a little secret. Your parents didn't tell you or show you everything that went on in their marriage. Hopefully you never saw your parents have sex, for example, but if you are sitting here and reading this, then obviously your parents had...you see where I'm going.

Notes

Notes

Don't make the mistake of comparing your marriage with other people's marriages. There are two things wrong with this: 1) You don't know everything that goes on in someone else's marriage, and 2) Another person's marriage is not the benchmark for marriage. God gave us the benchmark for marriage in Ephesians 5:22-33:

> Wives, submit yourselves to your own husbands as you do to the Lord. For the husband is the head of the wife as Christ is the head of the church, his body, of which he is the Savior. Now as the church submits to Christ, so also wives should submit to their husbands in everything.
>
> Husbands, love your wives, just as Christ loved the church and gave himself up for her to make her holy, cleansing her by the washing with water through the word, and to present her to himself as a radiant church, without stain or wrinkle or any other blemish, but holy and blameless.
>
> In this same way, husbands ought to love their wives as their own bodies. He who loves his wife loves himself. After all, no one ever hated their own body, but they feed and care for their body, just as Christ does the church—for we are members of his body. "For this reason a man will leave his father and mother and be united to his wife, and the two will become one flesh." This is a profound mystery—but I am talking about Christ and the church. However, each one of you also must love his wife as he loves himself, and the wife must respect her husband.

One Sunday morning, not long after we moved to Jackson, Mississippi, from Memphis, Tennessee, Teresa and I had a disagreement, conflict, argument, whatever you want to call it, before we arrived at church that morning (yes, marriage coaches and therapists do have disagreements). During the service, Teresa leaned over to me and said, "Put your arms around me. Everyone is going to think you are mad at me."

Session 3: Great Expectations

I'm normally very touchy feely. I like to sit as close as possible to my wife. I like to touch her, and hug her, so we sit really close together at church, and my arm is typically around her shoulder.

That particular morning, however, there was space between us and both of us knew this was not the norm, so Teresa leaned over and asked me to "go back to the norm."

My response was, "I am mad at you. I was mad when we got here. I'm mad now and I may be mad when we leave here." And although I didn't say this, I was actually thinking, *I absolutely will not pretend.*

The point of my story is if you see a couple who has what you think is the perfect marriage, with no conflicts, no problems, and no issues, that's because they are pretending!

Everyone does it. Right in the middle of a heated discussion, the phone rings and your angry voice magically melts and changes as you answer the phone, "Hello?" in a pleasant and sugary voice.

You know what I mean. I'm not suggesting you air your differences in public. I'm just saying couples have disagreements whether you see them or not.

Fairytale: Having children will bring us closer together.

Truth: In our 29 years of marriage, without a doubt, the most conflict we've had has been centered around our four children. We'll talk more about this in the session on parenting, but for now, trust us. While Psalm 127:3-5 teaches us that children are a blessing from God, they will not make a bad marriage better.

Children bring additional responsibilities, stressors, and issues that often magnify already-existing issues. We're not saying that you should wait until you have "fixed" all your problems to have children (because none of us would ever have children), but if you have the flu, for example, going to the movies won't make your illness better, and you will probably infect other people, as well.

Take a few minutes to write down some of the "fairytales" you have heard about marriage.

_____

_____

_____

_____

_____

_____

The institution of marriage is surrounded by a number of fairytales, myths, stories and advice freely offered by people on a daily basis. Unfortunately, many people listen to and believe these pieces of so-called wisdom to the point where they don't help their marriage and in fact, only hinder its growth. Many myths regarding relationships are incredibly damaging and it is unfortunate that many people hold the myths we have discussed here to be true.

Once you understand why certain bits of advice or information can be regarded as fairytales, you can break through what could be blocking the growth of your marriage. In fact, you may actually learn to appreciate your spouse and your role in your marriage even more.

Even though you will promise to love and cherish your spouse when you get married, most people actually mean, "I am really looking for someone who will love and cherish me."

What is the major difference in these two ways of thinking?

Marriage is not primarily about you. It's just as important to become the right person as it is to find the right person.

To listen to the podcast with Jim and Teresa discussing this session and additional resources, go to www.RelationshipSuccessUniversity.com/bookguide.

Session 4: Lose Your Mind If You Want to Love Your Spouse

You can't love your spouse the way God wants unless you decrease and allow Christ to increase. You need to make a switch!

Philippians 2: 5-10 (KJV) says:

> Let this mind be in you, which was also in Christ Jesus: Who, being in the form of God, thought it not robbery to be equal with God. But made himself of no reputation, and took upon him the form of a servant, and was made in the likeness of men: And being found in fashion as a man, he humbled himself, and became obedient unto death, even the death of the cross. Wherefore God also hath highly exalted him, and given him a name which is above every name: That at the name of Jesus every knee should bow, of things in heaven, and things in earth, and things under the earth;

Romans 12:1-3 (KJV) says:

> I beseech you therefore, brethren, by the mercies of God, that ye present your bodies a living sacrifice, holy, acceptable unto God, which is your reasonable service. And be not conformed to this world: but be ye transformed by the renewing of your mind, that ye may prove what is that good, and acceptable, and perfect, will of God. For I say, through the grace given unto me, to every man that is among you, not to think of himself more highly than he ought to think; but to think soberly, according as God hath dealt to every man the measure of faith.

You won't have a really great marriage unless you are out of your mind. This session is about discovering how to lose your mind and gain the best marriage ever. You cannot have a great marriage unless you lose (transform) your mind and replace it with the mind of Christ. That's why we say: "Lose Your Mind and Save Your Marriage."

A lot of people argue, "Being married to my spouse drove me out of my mind." Well let's reverse the process. Why not go out of your mind first in order to save your marriage? Marriage is the closest possible relationship between two depraved human beings. Thus, marriage is potentially a wonder of grace or the scene of intense pain. YOU DECIDE.

Having a super marriage begins with a supernatural transformation.

Rick Warren, author of *A Purpose Driven Life*, had this to say about marriage:

> Marriage is a life-long process designed to teach you to see the needs of another person as more important than your own. It's a difficult transition because it's not natural. To think this way requires an intentional shift that can be made only through the power of God in your life.

The reward, however, is greater than anything you could ever imagine. God's plan for your marriage is wider and deeper than anything in your wildest, craziest dreams.

In marriage we are asked to do things that are counter intuitive to our very natures, such as:

- Love another above ourselves.
- Endure in the midst of unpleasant situations.
- Be selfless instead of selfish.
- Nod our heads and say, "Yes, dear" when you really want to say, "That is the craziest thing I have ever heard."

As you can see, it is not possible to be the husbands, wives, fathers, or mothers we are meant to be unless our minds have been transformed.

Our youngest daughter, Elizabeth, speaks Spanish as well as you and I speak English. But when she speaks Spanish to me, I don't understand her because no one has ever trained me to speak Spanish. If a person has never been trained to speak another language, anything that person hears or reads in that language is incomprehensible. That is how this manual will seem to you unless you first learn to speak another language – the language of Christ. To speak the language of Christ, and really understand the language of Christ, you must first become like Christ. Are you a Christian?

When I was enrolled in seminary, I became really good friends with Arthur Toro. Arthur literally left everything and everyone he knew in Kenya to come to America to study.

One night I asked Arthur and his wife to come to a small group Bible study with Teresa and me. When we pulled up in front of the Family Life Center, Arthur's eyes got really big at the size of the structure and with his African accent he asked me one of the most important questions you can ask about the church: "How many Christians are here?"

Now what he thought he was asking and what he was really asking were two different questions.

He was really asking how many members we had, and as a member of the deacon ministry, I knew that answer: approximately 2,000 families, but his question was:

How many Christians are here?

I turned to Arthur and said, "That's a really good question. I don't know."

Okay, now let me ask another question. This is a different question than "Are you a Christian?" This is a deeper question, a penetrating question, a probing question, and a telling question.

Have you come to the place in your spiritual life, where if you were to die today, you would know for certain that you would go to heaven?

Notes

Now keep in mind, death is not an "if" but a "when." Unless Jesus comes back first, all of us are going to die (at least temporarily, but I will get to that later).

If you die tonight, are you certain beyond a shadow of a doubt that you are going to heaven?

Just in case you are confused, going to heaven is one of the perks of being a Christian, so you should have an answer. As a matter of fact, let's pause until you answer.

When I ask that question I get one of 4 responses:

_____ Yes

_____ No

_____ Not sure

_____ I didn't think anyone could really be sure

Please check your appropriate answer. This is the most important question you will ever be asked. Let's say you answered "Yes." My follow up questions would be:

If you were to die tonight and stand before God and He asked you, "Why should I let you into heaven?" what would you say?

Some possible answers:

____ I have tried to live the best life I could.

____ I am not really a bad person.

____ I grew up in a Christian home.

____ I grew up going to church.

Really think and write your answer below or check one of the answers above if it applies.

_____

_____

Session 4: Lose Your Mind If You Want to Love Your Spouse

Let me attempt to explain the Gospel and the plan of salvation in writing.

This is an actual conversation I had with Angel (that's her real name; I promise)

Me: If you were to die tonight, are you certain you would go to heaven?

Angel: I'm not sure that anyone can really know.

Me: Really? You know, that's just the way I felt about it. For many years I didn't know. But I have some great news. I discovered it is possible to know, and there are a great number of people who know. In fact, I learned that "knowing" was the reason the Bible was written. 1 John 5:13 says, "These things have I written unto you that ye believe on the name of the Son of God; that ye may know that ye have eternal life, and that ye may believe on the name of the Son of God."

Angel: I never knew the Bible said that.

Me: Think how wonderful it would be if you could go to bed tonight and lay your head on the pillow, knowing for certain that if you don't wake up in your bedroom, you will wake up in heaven with Jesus Christ. Would you like for me to share with you how I made that discovery and how you can know it, too?

Angel: Yes, please do.

Me: Ok. I have some really good news for you. Let's start with grace. Heaven is a free gift, at least it's free to us. Jesus did pay for it with his life by dying on the cross. For years I thought heaven was something I had to earn by keeping the commandments, being "good," going to church, and basically doing more good than I did bad. I had a scale in my mind and if the good stuff I did outweighed the bad stuff I did, I would get to heaven. In truth, a person cannot do enough good stuff

Notes

to earn his or her way into heaven. GRACE is God's unmerited favor. It's unearned, undeserved, and unmerited. You have probably been told before that nothing is free. We always look for the catch. But thank God the greatest thing man could ever have is FREE to us. It wasn't free to the Giver – we will cover that later – but it is free to us.

The first thing we need to understand is what the Bible says about you and me. Romans 3:10 and 23 says, "There is none righteous, no not one…for all have sinned and come short of the glory of God. And Isaiah 53:6 says, "There is not a just man upon the face of the earth that doeth good and sinneth not. We have turned everyone to his own way." So the Bible teaches that all of us have sinned. Are we together so far?

Angel: Yes.

Me: Sin is not just the major things we think about – murder, stealing, lying, fornication, adultery, etc. Sin is even an evil or impure thought.

Jesus said that a sin in thought is the same "wrong" as a sin in deed. Matthew 5:21-22 says, "Ye have heard it said…whosoever shall kill shall be in danger of the judgment…but I say that whosoever is angry with this brother without cause shall be in danger of the judgment."

I went on to answer all of Angel's questions, explaining the Gospel and the plan of salvation, and when I left, Angel had the assurance that when she dies she will spend eternity in heaven. The following is the abbreviated form of what I spent an hour or more talking with Angel about:

THE GOSPEL (Gospel Means "Good News")

A. **Grace**: Heaven is a <u>free gift</u>. It is not earned nor deserved. This can be seen more clearly when we understand what the Bible says about man in Romans 6:23 and Ephesians 2:8-9.

Session 4: Lose Your Mind If You Want to Love Your Spouse

B. **Man**: is a sinner and cannot save himself. This comes into sharper focus when we look at what the Bible says about God in Romans 3:23, Romans 5:12, & Proverbs 14:12.

C. **God**: is merciful and therefore does not want to punish us, but He is also just and therefore must punish our sin. God solved this problem through sacrificing <u>Jesus Christ</u>. See Romans 5:8 and Romans 6:23.

D. **Christ**: is the infinite God-man. He died to pay for our sins and to purchase a place in heaven for us, which He <u>offers</u> as a <u>gift</u>. This gift is received by faith. See John. 1:1, 14; 1 Peter 2:24; and 2 Corinthians 5:21.

E. **Faith**: is not mere intellectual assent or temporal faith. It is trusting in <u>Jesus Christ</u> alone for our salvation. See James 2:19, Romans 10:9, and Ephesians 2:8-10.

THE COMMITMENT

A. **Qualifying question**: Does this make sense to you?

B. **Commitment question**: Would you like to receive the gift of eternal life? See John 1:12.

C. **Clarification of commitment**: This is the most important decision a person can ever make, so let me clarify it for you again. You receive eternal life by transferring your trust to the resurrected and living Christ. You must receive Him as your Savior and your Lord. You must repent and want to become a responsible member in God's family forever. Is this what you want?

D. **Prayer of commitment**: If this is really what you want, you can pray. Tell God what you now understand and have decided. Be assured that God loves you and wants to forgive, save, and heal you. Cast all your burdens on Him, and embrace

Jesus with all your heart. Pray this prayer, mean it, and you will be saved, right where you sit. Repeat this prayer:

> LORD here and now I repent and believe in Jesus Christ, the Son of God. I believe Jesus died for me, as my Substitute, and rose from the dead according to the Scriptures. Even though I was apart from you, separated by my sin, Jesus saw me, helpless and fallen, and loved me enough to die for me.
>
> I believe that Jesus suffered the penalty for all my sins. He paid the full price to wipe out my debt. Because Jesus took my punishment, I am now free. No sin remains to condemn me. I'm no longer guilty before God. I can never be judged or condemned for my sins because they were judged in Jesus.
>
> I believe that this Good News, and the message of the Cross is true. I trust your promise that everyone who asks receives. Please forgive me, Lord. I receive you now into my heart.
>
> I accept your gracious gift of love, mercy, and peace.
>
> The LORD Jesus Christ now lives in me.
>
> I am a new creation in Christ, born of God with the life of Jesus in me.
>
> My record is wiped clean because of your grace and mercy.

E. If you repeated this prayer and you were sincere (now you can have that assurance) I would like you to read something important that Jesus says about what you have just done. Read John 6:47, Romans 10:13, and 2 Corinthians 5:17.

Now that your mind has been transformed, now that you have the mind of Christ, we can continue.

In your own words what does it mean to have the mind of Christ?

_____

_____

Why is it important to have the mind of Christ?

_____

_____

Can you really be effective as a husband or wife in your "own mind"?

_____

_____

 To listen to the podcast with Jim and Teresa discussing this session and additional resources, go to www.RelationshipSuccessUniversity.com/bookguide.

I Heard a Knock

It was a quiet morning not a sound could be heard

Except for the occasional sound of a chirping bird

All of a sudden I heard a knock

Who could this be, it's only 8 o'clock

Oh it's only me he said with a smile

Can you come next door and talk for a while

I said I could and with that we sat down

And boy was my heart starting to pound

He asked me a question very discreetly

And who would have thought it would change my life completely

He asked me if I died, was I sure where my soul would go

I hated to say it but the truthful answer was no

He asked me to bow my head and he said a special prayer

And I gave Jesus all my sins and burdens to bear

As he finished the prayer and we raised our heads

I felt better because of what he had said

I know now where I'll be when I die

I'll have a place with Jesus in his mansion on high

So now I would like to say to the man who changed my life

Thank you Jim for sharing Jesus Christ

- Angel Lovern -

May 16, 2005

Session 5: Do You Know What You Are About To Do? Covenant or Contract?

Since marriage is a covenant, I have no choice but to be committed 'til death do us part.

Have you ever heard the phrase "burn the ships"? It comes from a historic conquest in 1519 when Spanish Conquistador Hernando Cortez landed in Mexico on the shores of the Yucatan, with only one objective – to seize the great treasures known to be there, hoarded by the Aztecs. Cortez was committed to his mission and his quest for riches is legendary.

Cortez was an excellent motivator. He convinced more than 500 soldiers and 100 sailors to set sail from Spain to Mexico, commanding 11 ships, to take the world's richest treasure. The historic question is, "How did a small band of Spanish soldiers arrive in a strange country and swiftly bring about the overthrow of a large empire that had been in power for more than six centuries?"

For Cortez, the answer was easy. It was all or nothing! It was a complete and total commitment. To get the "buy in" from the rest of his men, Cortez took away the option of failure. It was conquer, be heroes, and enjoy the spoils of victory…or DIE! When Cortez and his men arrived on the shores of the Yucatan, he rallied the men for one final pep talk before leading them into battle and uttered these three words that changed the course of history: "Burn the ships."

But his men resisted. So Cortez repeated, "Burn the ships!" He then uttered these words: "If we are going home, we are going home in their ships." With that, Cortez and his men burned their own ships. Doing so raised the commitment of the men to a level much higher than any of them, including Cortez, could have ever imagined.

Amazingly, the men conquered the Aztecs and succeeded in something where others had been unsuccessful for six centuries. With the victory, Cortez and his men took the treasure. Why did they win? They had no escape, no fallback position. They had no choice! It was "succeed or die." Their ships were burned. They had no way to get back. Their backs were against the wall.

To "really succeed" you must have an attitude much like that of Cortez and his men. They did not have a "crutch" or "fallback position." They frankly didn't have any options. Pretty strong position, isn't it? How would you like to be fighting someone with that level of motivation and commitment?

A contract is a bi-lateral agreement that says, "If you do this, I will do that," while a covenant is a unilateral agreement that says, "I agree to do this no matter what you do or don't do."
That's the difference. In a covenant, I focus on the promise I made, not the promises that may or may not have been made to me. In a covenant, I focus on my responsibility, not the responsibilities others may or may not be living up to.

1. When is it okay to get a divorce?

_____

_____

2. What does the Bible say about divorce? Read 1 Corinthians 7:15, Matthew 5:32, & Matthew 19:8

_____

_____

3. How long do you expect to be married?

_____

_____

4. What are some characteristics of marriage within your family?

_____

_____

A covenant is different from a "promise," a "suggestion" or a "good idea."

Covenant, as defined by the Scriptures, is a solemn and binding relationship that is meant to last a lifetime. When we come to know the biblical truth that a covenant involves a "walk into death," it produces a supernatural oneness between covenant partners and ultimately withholds nothing from God. This truth will set us free (See John 8:36), free to live as we should in our marriages, and not to live as we please.

Dennis Rainey, a well-known Christian family life speaker, writes:

> For the past two years I have had a growing concern that the Christian community has passively watched the "dumbing down" of **the marriage covenant**. Marriage has become little more than an upgraded social contract between two people—not **a holy covenant between a man and a woman and their God for a lifetime**. In the Old Testament days, a covenant was solemn and binding.
>
> When two people entered into a covenant with one another, a goat or lamb would be slain and its carcass would be cut in half. With the two halves separated and lying on the ground, the two people who had formed the covenant would solemnize their promise by walking between the two halves. "May God do so to me [cut me in half] if I ever break this covenant with you and God!" You get the feeling that a covenant in those days had just a little more substance than today."

RC Sproul adds that:

> **People are no longer familiar with the nature of covenants.** Covenants establish relationships publicly and create accountability. If two people are simply living together, either spouse may abandon the other without accountability. The covenant involves a promise to obey God and to be faithful—and also involves a curse: May God

judge me if I break this pledge. **People avoid the covenant of marriage because they want to have irresponsible relationships,** but such relationships are hazardous to human life. God has created us so that we blossom as human beings when we conform to God's covenantal structures.

When we live irresponsibly, we destroy ourselves and others...**Living by covenants is God's method to anchor our lives and provide security against the prevailing cultural disintegration.**

Divorce is not an Option!

Understand and agree to this before you are married!

A covenant in the Bible clearly represents a serious commitment between two parties. The covenant between Jacob and Laban was so serious that God was called to serve as a witness, according to Genesis 31:43-55. In view of the divinely ordained nature of the covenant of marriage, it, too, is a solemn, binding agreement witnessed by the attendees.

Sadly, too few married couples or wedding witnesses understand the seriousness of the covenant or of their roles as lifelong witnesses.

If you have a history of failed marriages in your immediate or extended family, what are you going to do differently? How will your marriage survive when so many others have failed?

_____

_____

_____

Session 5: Do You Know What You Are About To Do? Covenant Or Contract?

Jack Hayford writes:

> The **covenant of marriage** is the single most important human bond that holds all of God's work on the planet together. It is no small wonder that the Lord is passionate about the sanctity of marriage and the stability of the home. This **covenant of marriage** is based on the covenant God has made with us. It is in the power of His promise to mankind that our personal **covenant of marriage** can be kept against the forces that would destroy homes and ruin lives.

Matthew Henry adds:

> In ancient times, **covenant** was the most <u>**solemn and binding**</u> agreement into which two parties could enter. It is tragic that this vital truth seems to have been lost in much of our modern culture, including even in the church, with devastating consequences to American families.... It is, therefore, critical that one understand the truth about covenant, as it relates to marriage.

R C Sproul further elaborates on the covenant of marriage in the following excerpt:

> First, **marriage is a covenant.** This is the keystone of the analogy Paul makes in Ephesians 5 between earthly marriage and the relationship between Christ and the church. The bond between Jesus and His bride forms the New Covenant, the spiritual reality of which human marriages are a type. <u>Malachi 2:14</u> **explicitly** makes the connection between **marriage and covenant**. But what does that mean? We should consider several aspects of a covenant.
>
> **First, a covenant establishes a bond between two parties,** in this case the husband and wife. At the heart of this bond is a promise, the promise of faithfulness.
>
> **Second, a covenant establishes obligations.** A primary obligation in marriage is fidelity. The husband is obligated to lead his wife in love, and she is obligated to submit to him in the fear of the Lord.

Notes

Third, a covenant is public. It is contracted before witnesses. There is a great difference between the whispered pledges of a boy in the back seat of a car and the solemn vows of a young man before God and witnesses in the ceremony of holy matrimony. This public character of the covenant means that marriage is a social institution that society has an interest in preserving. As an institution, marriage is regulated by the Word of God. That the marriage covenant is not simply a private affair becomes clear when we consider divorce.

Divorce wrecks the lives of children. Divorce destroys peace of mind and damages the effectiveness of employees. Divorce upsets friends and family. For Christians, an ungodly divorce forces the elders of the church to exercise discipline. Marriage is the closest possible relationship between two depraved human beings. Thus, marriage is potentially a wonder of grace or the scene of intense pain.

IN THE COVENANT OF MARRIAGE REMEMBER THE FOLLOWING TRUTHS...

1) TWO LIVES BECOME ONE

In a covenant you become identified with the other individual and there is a supernatural joining of lives (**two** becoming **one**). It is a mystery but it is an illustration of the way Christ & the church are one. (Ephesians 5:32)

In marriage, your family becomes your spouse's family, your desires become your beloved's desires, and yes, even your finances become your covenant partner's finances (including credit card bills).

2) THERE IS A SIGN TO REMEMBER THAT SERVES AS A WITNESS AND A MEMORIAL

When God entered a covenant with Noah, He gave Noah the rainbow, which was to be a testimony that God would remain forever faithful and keep the covenant never again to flood the earth to destroy all flesh.

In Genesis 9:16 the LORD God testified that...

When the (rain) **bow** is in the cloud, then I will look upon it, to remember the everlasting covenant between God and every living creature of all flesh that is on the earth.

When you enter into a covenant with your beloved, the sign is usually a **RING**, which serves as a constant reminder (memorial) of the solemn and binding of your marriage covenant.

3) THERE IS A CHANGE IN NAME

In Genesis 17:5, 15 when God reaffirmed His covenant with Abram, God said, "No longer shall your name be called **Abram**, but your name shall be **Abraham**; for I will make you the father of a multitude of nations, as for **Sarai** your wife, you shall not call her name Sarai, but **Sarah** shall be her name.

As the wife takes on her husband's name, this change symbolizes the supernatural **identity** and **oneness** God intended for the people who entered the marriage covenant.

4) THERE IS A MEAL SHARED

Biblical covenants were often commemorated with a "covenant meal." The most famous covenant meal is of course found in the New Covenant where we read that the Lord Jesus on the night He was betrayed took bread and when He had given thanks, He broke it and said, "This is My body, which is for you; do this in remembrance of Me." In the same way He took the cup also, after supper, saying, "This cup is the NEW COVENANT IN MY BLOOD; do this as often as you drink it in remembrance of Me. (1 Corinthians 11:24, 25)

In a short while you will probably celebrate your New Covenant relationship by feeding each other wedding cake, which is a picture that you are now **sharing a**

common life, that two lives have become one.

5) THERE IS A FRIEND WHO WILL STICK CLOSER THAN A BROTHER

Friend is a covenant term and is beautifully seen in God's covenant with Abraham.

James underscores the association of **"covenant"** and **"friend,"** writing that when Abraham offered up Isaac, his son, on the altar, his faith was shown to be in accordance with his works and thus...

In Genesis, God declared to His covenant partner and "friend":

Shall I hide (keep secret, conceal, cover) from Abraham what I am about to do, since Abraham will surely become a great and mighty nation, and in him all the nations of the earth will be blessed?" (Genesis 18:17,18)

Abraham was the friend of God by virtue of entering covenant with Him. As friends in the marriage covenant there should be no secrets kept or concealed from the covenant partner.

6) THERE ARE WITNESSES TO TESTIFY

In the Old Testament, the solemnity of cutting a covenant was often witnessed by setting up a memorial or sign. Similarly, when a man and a woman enter into the solemn, binding covenant of marriage, witnesses are present, the highest of which is God Himself. Covenant in the Bible clearly represents a serious commitment between two parties.

The covenant between Jacob and Laban was so serious that God was called to serve as a witness! In view of the divinely ordained nature of the covenant of marriage, it too is a solemn, binding agreement that is witnessed by the attendees. Sadly, too few married couples or wedding witnesses have a sense of the seriousness of the covenant or of their roles as lifelong witnesses.

7) THERE IS A COVENANT PARTNER TO DEFEND

We see this principle of covenant vividly illustrated in the covenant David cut with Saul's son, Jonathan. In this exchange we see that covenant is stronger than paternal ties (Jonathan was more committed to his covenant partner, David, than to his father, King Saul!) and stronger than personal ambition. (Jonathan would have been next in line to be king but willingly released that right to his covenant partner, David!)

Therefore, when two people or parties entered into covenant, they understood that everything they had was now held in common, even each other's enemies (credit card debts, etc.). Whenever one was under attack, it was the duty of the other to come to his aid.

What were David and Jonathan saying?

They were saying, "Because you and I are no longer living independent lives, but are in covenant – and because covenant is the most solemn, binding agreement that can be made between two parties – I am bound by covenant to defend you from your enemies. Those who attack you become my enemies."

Do you clearly understand the difference between a covenant and a contract?

_____ Yes _____ No

What are some of the differences?

_____

_____

Would you prefer a covenant marriage or a contract marriage?

_____ Covenant _____ Contract

Why?

_____

_____

Now that you understand the seriousness of a covenant marriage, do you understand what you are about to do?

_____ Yes _____ No

Explain:

_____

_____

While a marriage is a legal contract to be honored and informal contracts within a marriage often help us effectively use our different skills to our mutual benefit, a Christian marriage is much more than a contract. This "much more" is to be discovered in the word "covenant."

Session 5: Do You Know What You Are About To Do? Covenant Or Contract?

According to Dr. Gary Chapman, there are 5 general characteristics of contracts:

1. Contracts are often made for a limited period of time.
2. Contracts most often deal with specific actions.
3. Contracts are based on an if-then mentality.
4. Contracts are motivated by the desire to get something we want.
5. Contracts are sometimes unspoken and implicit.

The first time covenant is used in the Bible is Genesis 6:18. Marriage is called a covenant in Malachi 2:14.

There are also 5 general characteristics of covenants:

1. Covenants are initiated for the benefit of the other person.
2. In covenant relationships, people make unconditional promises.
3. Covenant relationships are based on steadfast love.
4. Covenant relationships view commitments as permanent.
5. Covenant relationships require confrontation and forgiveness.

How Do You Stay Committed to the Covenant and Not Be Miserable in the Marriage?

We added this session to our book after we received a simple, yet profound, question from one of our couples during a weekend premarital intensive. We had just completed the previous session on "Covenant vs. Contract" marriages when the young lady said:

Now I understand the difference between contract and covenant. I understand it is God's plan for me to be married until death, so my question is, how can I honor the covenant, stay married, and also be excited and happy about being married?

Notes

As the young lady revealed more about herself during the session, we discovered she had observed many examples of wives "suffering in silence" through really bad marriages and yet remaining in them strictly out of a sense of duty to the covenant, the institution of marriage, and the family. She did not want to have this kind of marriage, nor did we want her to have this kind of marriage.

While honoring the vow you are making to stay married until death will require a sense of duty, or, as we described in Session Two, a transforming of the mind, your marriage should also be fun and enjoyable. You should actually enjoy coming home and spending time with the person you have pledged to spend the rest of your life with.

So how can you do that? The ultimate answer to that question is spiritual growth and maturity, though there are also some practical things you can do to make your marriage enjoyable and exciting.

The excerpts below are taken from the writings and teachings of Dr. Willard Harley:

One thing we need to understand is what makes a marriage work. Often we are so preoccupied with what causes them to fail, (preventative work) that we overlooked what helped them succeed (proactive work). When most couples are asked why they got married in the first place, it wasn't because of great communication or great conflict-resolving skills (although both are very important). It was because they were in love. In miserable marriages, over the years, they somehow lost their love for each other. In fact, some had even come to hate each other.

When couples were asked what it would take for them to be happily married again, most couldn't imagine that ever happening. As couples reflect on it, they come to the realization that they would need to be in love again.

With this insight, couples can attack emotional issues not just rational issues. Couples who focus on making sure the emotional feeling of love is constant, rather than focusing on resolving conflicts and restoring communication, end up in much more fulfilling relationships. If a couple knew how to restore love, then conflicts might not be as much of an issue.

Psychology teaches us that learned associations trigger most of our emotional reactions. Whenever something is presented repeatedly with a physically induced emotion, it tends to trigger that emotion all by itself. For example, if you flash the color blue along with an electric shock, and the color red with a soothing back rub, eventually the color blue will tend to upset you and the color red will tend to relax you.

Applying the same principle to the feeling of love, theorize that love might be nothing more than a learned association. If someone were to be present often enough when you were feeling particularly good, the person's presence in general might be enough to trigger that good feeling – something known as the feeling of love.

By encouraging each spouse to try to do whatever it took to make each other happy, and avoid doing what made each other unhappy, that feeling of love would be restored.

Obviously when dealing with fallen and sinful human beings as we all are, we are going to fall short. That is where the grace of God comes in, but let's continue to focus on our feeble attempts to help the situation.

Ignorance often contributes to a couple's failure to care for one another. Both men and women tend to try to meet needs that they value. The problem is men's needs are often very different from women's needs, so both men and women waste efforts trying to meet the wrong needs.

The right needs are so strong that when they are not met in marriage, people are tempted to go outside marriage to satisfy them. Emotional needs should be met for the sake of care itself, however, and not just because of the risk of having an affair. Marriage is a very special relationship. Promises are made to allow a spouse the exclusive right to meet some of these important needs. When they are unmet, it is unfair to the spouse who must go through life without ethical alternatives.

Dr. Harley describes the ten emotional needs of men and women. He helps you identify which needs are most important to you and your spouse, helps each of you communicate them to one another, and helps you learn to meet them.

Successful marriages require skill – skill in caring for the one you promised to cherish throughout life. Good intentions are not enough. *His Needs, Her Needs* was written to educate you in the care of your spouse. Once you have learned its lessons, your spouse will find you irresistible, a condition that is essential to a happy and successful marriage.

To listen to the podcast with Jim and Teresa discussing this session and additional resources, go to www.RelationshipSuccessUniversity.com/bookguide.

Session 6: Communicate or Your Marriage Will Disintegrate

I know you believe you understand what you think I said, but I am not sure you realize what you thought you heard is not what I meant.

When a group of divorced couples were asked, "Why did your marriage fail?" 86% said, "Deficient communication."

An experiment was conducted to determine the average amount of conversation between husbands and wives in a typical week. Participants in the study wore microphones that recorded every word spoken. The average communication time was 17 minutes a week!

Can You Hear Me Now?

Studies show the average male uses about 12,000 words a day, the entire day. A woman, on the other hand, averages 25,000 words per day.

Think about how this statistic can affect a marriage. Case in point: Early in our marriage, Teresa was a stay-at-home mom and I made my living by talking (consulting) with people. By the time I came home, I had already used my "allotted" words for the day.

Teresa, on the other hand, was dying to talk because she had only used a small portion of her words for the day, and they were mostly used for "baby talk" because it's difficult to have adult conversation with 3-month-old twins. Often times the minute I stepped in the door, Teresa began to unload.

Understanding this scientific fact, however, helped me cope with her need to talk and my need not to talk. As a result, I became a lot more sensitive to her need for conversation, and I even called home sometimes 3 or 4 times a day just to talk. In short, I made a commitment to communicate.

Do you understand how not knowing this information can lead to frustration? Note to men. Your job does not stop when you get home. On the contrary, your most important jobs as husband and father start when you walk in the door.

God designed marriage to be the most intimate of human relationships, but such intimacy cannot be obtained without wholesome, responsible communication. We must identify the negative patterns of communication that keep us from intimacy and build positive patterns that will draw us together.

> "...Communication is the primary vehicle by which two become one in the marriage relationship..."
>
> -- Dr. Gary Chapman

Read Ephesians 4:29-30.

1. What does this verse suggest about how we should communicate?

_____

_____

_____

2. How often do you communicate with your spouse-to-be on the following issues? Beside each category, place an "O" for often, an "S" for seldom, or an "N" for never.

Family matters/parenting _____ Friends _____ Dreams _____ Finances _____ Spiritual issues _____
Plans and goals _____ Sex _____ Current events _____ TV or Movies _____ Children _____

3. How would you grade yourself? Are you comfortable discussing peripheral issues and uncomfortable discussing issues of substance?

_____

_____

_____

There is no way your marriage can be what it should be unless you and your mate learn to communicate!

Session 6: Communicate or Your Marriage Will Disintegrate

Ever notice how in a battle the opposing side attempts to cut off communication? That's because if the two sides can't talk to one another, they end up detached, disorganized, discouraged, and ultimately defeated.

Satan works to cut off communication in a marriage in order to defeat you.

The Family – God's Smallest Battle Formation

Discuss how your marriage is like a small army – not you against one another, but you and your spouse (and later your children) against the world.

Communication between husband and wife is crucial if you are to survive and thrive in this fallen world where all outside communication works to destroy what God has communicated to you about marriage.

How do outside influences and messages work to affect communication in a marriage?

_____

_____

_____

_____

Who is the Master Communicator? Jesus Christ. This makes Jesus both the pattern and the power behind good communication.

Notes

Read 1 Peter 2:21-24.

There are 6 reasons why we communicate. Each reason represents a level of progress into deeper intimacy. A break at any level sets the couple back to the previous (lower) level:

1. Basic information – news, weather, sports, and current events
2. Basic requests – "I need you to pick up the dry cleaning"; "We are out of milk."
3. Conflict resolution – usually turns into yelling and screaming or silence
4. Connecting with each other – ideas, judgments, philosophies, and goals
5. Sharing personal information – "This is how I really feel."
6. Intimate communication – holding nothing back: hurts, fears, wounds, our deepest thoughts, and things most people will never know

I heard Jimmy Evans of www.MarriageToday.tv say "There are five standards for successful and effective communication."

Caring – "I care for you and, therefore, I care about what you are saying." It's impossible to communicate with a person who does not care. More about this under "Validation."

Praise – Positive and not negative language. People close off to negative language. To offer constructive criticism, you must first earn trust and trust is earned after the other person believes you have his or her best interests at heart. Your marriage will only go as high as the words you speak to your mate.

Truth – Proverbs 3:3 and Ephesians 4:15: Not verbalizing the truth often leads to passive-aggressive behavior and pent-up anger. Don't pretend. Be honest.

Faith – Speak the truth and have faith that God will handle everything. Speaking the truth over and over again (i.e., "nagging") is not effective. Stop trying to fix your spouse. Speak the truth, but don't speak it over and over again on the same issue.

Surrender – My tongue is surrendered to Almighty God and therefore I will let no unwholesome words come out of my mouth! "Sticks and stones may break my bones, but your words will never hurt" is a childish rhyme and a lie! Words do hurt!

I LUV You

Teresa and I are certified *Smalley Marriage Intensive Coaches!* The Smalley family founded the Smalley Marriage and Family Center and the "Marriage Restoration Intensive" in 2005. The center trains couples on how to effectively communicate in their marriages. They call the key to effective marriage communication "*LUV Talk* – The Most Powerful Communication Tool on Earth." *LUV Talk* means to Listen, Understand, and Validate.

Teresa and I have used this approach for years (although we had no formal name for it), and we think there is much to be learned from this method.

Listen – Listening is a skill that we're in danger of losing in a world of digital distraction and information overload. We listen with our body language, our eyes, our tones of voice, and our hearts. Listening is not just a function of our ears, but of our whole being. When you listen, you're not waiting for an opening to have your turn. You put your feelings, perceptions, and needs on hold while you work to fulfill the other person's need to be heard.

<u>**James 1:19**</u> – Wherefore, my beloved brethren, let every man be swift to hear, slow to speak, slow to wrath

<u>**Proverbs 18:13**</u> – He that answereth a matter before he heareth [it], it [is] folly and shame unto him.

<u>**Revelation 2:7**</u> – He that hath an ear, let him hear what the Spirit saith unto the churches; To him that overcometh will I give to eat of the tree of life, which is in the midst of the paradise of God.

Proverbs 25:12 – [As] an earring of gold, and an ornament of fine gold, [so is] a wise reprover upon an obedient ear.

Understand – How do you get understanding? First you ask God for it. Prayer has to be the centerpiece of a successful marriage. Second, you ask questions. When you are listening to your spouse and he or she says something you do not understand, ask questions.

Ask clarifying questions, such as:

- "What I heard you say was...is that correct?"
- "I hear you saying that…."
- "Are you saying…?"
- "So what you are saying is…." (Summarize)
- "So what you just said was…." (Repeat)

Often in the middle of a conversation, I will ask Teresa a clarifying question only to discover what she thinks she just said and what I actually heard are two entirely different things. Why does this happen? Because men and women are different.

I realize you learned that at an early age, but the major differences between men and women are not physical; they are psychological, emotional, and mental. We communicate and process information in different ways. And after 29 years of marriage, if we are still working to communicate better, you know you have a lot of work to do!

Stop now and replay a recent conversation, discussion, or disagreement. This time use clarifying questions as you're having the conversation to enhance communication between the two of you.

Typically my clarifying questions start with, "Now this is what I heard you say. Is that in fact what you are actually saying?"

Teresa often responds with, "No, that is not at all what I just said."

She may then repeat a previous statement. But this time, I have used my clarifying question as a measuring tool to see how much or how little of her intended meaning I actually understood.

On the subject of clarifying questions, the Smalleys say:

> One of the biggest, most loving things you can do while trying to seek understanding is to ask clarifying questions. A clarifying question gives the customer a true sense of validation and value. Clarifying questions are an incredible way to let your spouse know that you care very deeply about your marriage. A clarifying question is important when your spouse makes a general statement like, "I need more time together."
>
> Well, what in the world does that mean? It is too general a statement and needs to be followed by a clarifying question like, "I hear that you want us to spend more time together, but what would spending more time together look like to you?"

Ephesians 1:18 — The eyes of <u>your</u> understanding being enlightened; that ye may know what is the hope of his calling, and what the riches of the glory of his inheritance in the saints,

Proverbs 3:5 — Trust in the LORD with all thine heart; and lean not unto thine own understanding.

Validate — *Wikipedia* defines validation as, "The reciprocated communication of respect which communicates that the other person's opinions are acknowledged, respected, heard, and (regardless whether or not the listener actually agrees with the content), they are being treated with genuine respect as a legitimate expression of their feelings, rather than marginalized or dismissed."

Notes

Validation is not about agreeing with what the other person has said; validation is about "repeating" what the other person has said, allowing both the speaker and the listener to determine if they are sending and receiving the same message.

What you are validating is the person's feelings, not necessarily agreeing with the content of his or her statement.

Michael and Amy Smalley continue:

> When you validate someone's feelings, you are honoring the person and your relationship over your right to judge.
>
> The fundamentals of validation are:
>
> - Acknowledge the other person's feelings.
> - Identify the feelings by asking specific questions or repeating specific statements.
> - Offer to listen, which means stopping any other activity and giving your spouse your undivided attention.
> - Help your spouse clearly define his or her feelings by rewording and repeating what you hear.
> - Be patient when your spouse is sharing; don't rush him or her through the sharing process.
>
> Another way to remember these directions to effective communication is:
>
> - Concentration (Really Listen)
> - Clarification (Really Understand)
> - Consideration (Really Validate)

Read and discuss the following:

The Awesome Power of Communication (1 Peter 2:21-23; James 3:1-10)

   A. The tongue gives direction. (James 3:4)
   B. The tongue brings destruction. (James 3:6)
   C. The tongue brings defilement. (James 3:8)

The Agonizing Problems in Communication

   A. We lack communication skills.
   B. Self-centeredness (1 Peter 2:24)
   C. Bitterness, unresolved problems and unforgiving spirits (1 Peter 2:22-23; Hebrews 12:15)
   D. The distractions of life (1 Peter 2:25, 3:11)
   E. The differences in temperaments
   F. Insecurity and fear (1 Peter 3:8)

The Amazing Approach to Proper Communication

   A. Husbands, learn to be more sensitive. (1 Peter 3:7)
   B. Both partners, deal with self-centeredness. (1 Peter 3:8)
   C. Be willing to overlook your partner's problems.
   D. If your partner has a closed spirit, try to find out why. (1 Peter 3:11)
   E. Create areas of commonality.
   F. Make time for communication. (1 Peter 3:11)

I want to reiterate that some of the most frustrating issues surrounding communication in marriage come from the fact that men and women are different. Since we are different, we think differently, we see differently, and we process information differently. Why? Because God made us different in order to make us one.

Notes

Some of the obvious differences that surface when two people are living in close quarters and attempting to communicate are:

- Men take risks; women want security.
- Men see the big picture; women see the details.
- Men want success; women want security.
- Men are protectors, so they are more suspicious and cautious with other people.
- Women are nurturers, so they tend to be more accepting and forgiving.
- Men primarily think logically with their heads; women primarily think (you think I am going to say "illogically," but I'm not) emotionally with their hearts.

Neither is right and neither is wrong; they both need each other.

Communication Assessment

Place a T for "True" or an F for "False" beside each statement.

____ I understand the importance of listening, and that listening is actually a way of ministering.

____ When someone is speaking to me, I give him or her my full attention.

____ When I enter a conversation, I am willing to admit that I may be wrong and I am willing to openly listen, learn, and evaluate what I hear.

____ I anticipate what I think you are about to say and finish your sentences for you.

____ I don't make quick, disingenuous apologies.

____ When another person is speaking, I don't interrupt.

____ When another person is speaking, I only interrupt to ask for clarification about something he or she said.

____ If I am not ready or willing to engage in conversation, I am committed to setting a time to reengage, and I stick to that time.

____ After someone has spoken, I can accurately summarize what the person has said.

Session 6: Communicate or Your Marriage Will Disintegrate

____ I am open to constructive criticism, and when I ask a question, I really want the truth.

____ I tend to clam up and go silent rather than communicate.

____ I am not able to communicate on certain issues without becoming loud and angry.

____ Sometimes I intentionally say things to hurt my spouse and make him or her feel bad.

Turn to your spouse and ask, "Do you think I am a good listener? What can I do to be a better listener?"

_____

_____

_____

Switch assessments, review your spouse's answers, and mark either A for "Agree" or D for "Disagree."

Remember LUV Talk? Can you summarize what your spouse just told you?

_____

_____

_____

Are you willing to make a concerted effort to improve?

_____

_____

_____

Communication is difficult and nearly impossible if you are not speaking the same language as your spouse. Everyone agrees that communication is essential to a healthy marriage, but how do we communicate?

___

___

___

Is what I think I'm saying to my spouse what he or she is really hearing?

___

___

___

Everyone communicates in a different love language! What is your language and what is your spouse's?

___

___

___

Most of us grow up learning the language of our parents, grandparents, and people we spend time with, and that language becomes our native tongue. Later we may learn additional languages, but usually that requires much more effort. It's the same with the language of love.

Yours and your spouse's emotional love language may be as different as Chinese is from English. No matter how hard you try to express love in English, if your spouse only understands Chinese, you and your spouse will never understand how to love each other.

The best resource we can recommend to help you learn to communicate effectively with your spouse is the work done by Dr. Gary Chapman. Dr. Chapman teaches us that falling in love is easy. Maintaining healthy relationships, on the other hand, is a daily, lifelong pursuit, but it doesn't have to be that hard. Once you know your "love language," you'll understand why some attempts at romance work, while others fall flat.

Dr. Gary Chapman's perennial *New York Times* bestseller, *The 5 Love Languages*® is full of "Aha!" moments that make expressing love easier and more desirable. You'll find yourself more motivated and more confident that you can succeed in having the relationships you've always wanted. More than 8 million copies have been sold!

The 5 Love Languages® debuted in 1992, and has helped countless couples identify practical and powerful ways to communicate love, simply by using the appropriate love language. Many husbands and wives who spent years struggling through marriages they thought were loveless discovered they had long been showing love through messages that weren't getting through to their spouses. By recognizing their different love languages, however, these spouses witnessed the rebirth of the love they thought was gone for good.

Notes

The 5 Love Languages® has been translated into more than 40 languages and is healing marriages around the world!

Of the countless ways we can communicate love to one another, five key categories, or five love languages, have proven to be universal and comprehensive—everyone has a love language, and we all identify primarily with one of the following five:

Words of Affirmation

Actions don't always speak louder than words. If this is your love language, unsolicited compliments mean the world to you. Hearing the words "I love you" are important—hearing the reasons behind that love sends your spirit skyward. Insults can leave you shattered and are not easily forgotten.

Quality Time

In the vernacular of Quality Time, nothing says "I love you" like full, undivided attention. Being there for this type of person is critical, but really being there—with the TV off, fork and knife down, and all chores and tasks on standby—makes your significant other feel truly special and loved. Distractions, postponed dates, or the failure to listen can be especially hurtful.

Receiving Gifts

Don't mistake this love language for materialism; the receiver of gifts thrives on the love, thoughtfulness, and effort behind those gifts. If you speak this language, the perfect gift or gesture shows that you are known, you are cared for, and you are prized above whatever was sacrificed to bring the gift to you. A missed birthday, anniversary, or a hasty, thoughtless gift would be disastrous—so would the absence of everyday gestures.

Acts of Service

Can vacuuming the floors really be an expression of love? Absolutely! Anything you do to ease the burden of responsibilities weighing on an "Acts of Service" person will speak volumes. The words he or she most wants to hear are "Let me do that for you." Laziness, broken commitments, and making more work for speakers of this language tell them their feelings don't matter.

Physical Touch

This language isn't all about the bedroom. A person whose primary language is Physical Touch is, not surprisingly, very touchy. Hugs, pats on the back, holding hands, and thoughtful touches on the arm, shoulder, or face can all be ways to show excitement, concern, care, and love. Physical presence and accessibility are crucial, while neglect or abuse can be unforgivable and destructive.

Go to www.5lovelanguages.com and take the assessment to determine your love language.

Learn the language of your spouse and communicate in it often!

To listen to the podcast with Jim and Teresa discussing this session and additional resources, go to www.RelationshipSuccessUniversity.com/bookguide.

Session 7: Caring Enough to Embrace Conflict

The following is an excerpt from Diane Sollee of Smart Marriages:

The number one predictor of divorce is the habitual avoidance of conflict.

What's sad is the reason couples avoid conflict is because they believe it (conflict) causes divorce.

It's like the cartoon where the couple explains to the marriage counselor, "We never talk anymore. We figured out that's when we do all our fighting." In the beginning, we avoid conflict because we are in love and we believe that "staying in love" is about agreeing, about NOT fighting.

We're afraid that if we disagree – or fight – we'll run our marriage off into the ditch. We believe that if we've found our soulmate, we'll agree about most things – and certainly about the important things.

Later, we avoid conflict because when we finally do try to deal with our differences (talk about them) things get so out of hand and our fights so destructive and upsetting, that we simply shut down. After a few bad blow-ups we become determined to avoid conflict at any cost. And, we start wondering if we married the wrong person. We think to ourselves: it shouldn't be this hard.

Successful couples are those who know how to discuss their differences in ways that actually strengthen their relationship and improve intimacy.

Successful couples know how to contain their disagreements – how to keep their disagreements from spilling over and contaminating the rest of their relationship.

While it's true that we don't get married to handle conflict, if a couple doesn't know how – or learn how – to fight or manage their disagreements successfully, they won't be able to do all the other things they got married to do.

Put another way, it's hard to take her out to the ball game if you're not speaking. Couples are often so determined to avoid disagreements that they shut down – quit talking, quit loving.
Couples need to know what the research has found: that every happy, successful couple has approximately ten areas of "incompatibility" or disagreement that they will never resolve.

Successful couples learn how to manage their areas of disagreement and live life "around" them – to love in spite of their differences and to develop understanding and empathy for their partner's positions.

The divorce courts have it all wrong. "Irreconcilable differences" — like a bad knee or a chronic back — are not a reason to divorce. Irreconcilable differences are part of every good marriage. Successful couples learn to dance in spite of their differences. They gain comfort in knowing they know their partner, know which issues they disagree on and must learn to manage.

They also understand that if they switch partners they'll just get ten new areas of disagreement, and sadly, the most destructive will be about the children from their earlier relationships.

In addition to skills for handling disagreements, we also have to learn to welcome and embrace change. When we marry we promise to stay together till death us do part — but, we don't promise to stay the same. That would be deadly dull. We need skills and confidence to welcome, integrate, and negotiate change along the way.

The good news is that the skills or behaviors for handling disagreement and conflict, for integrating change, and for expressing love, intimacy, sex, support, and appreciation can all be learned. Couples can unlearn the behaviors that predict divorce — that destroy love — and replace them with behaviors that keep love alive. (Yes, in addition to learning how to manage disagreements and integrate change, it's also crucial to learn how to express love and appreciation.)

The creators of *Smart Marriages…The Coalition for Marriage, Family, and Couples Education* say:

One thing is certain — there will be conflict. A marriage relationship places two sinful people in a close relationship and asks them to do what is unnatural (which is why your mind must be transformed) and that is to operate in a selfless manner when your natural state is to be selfish. Disagreements are not necessarily bad. Disagreements, handled properly, offer a great opportunity for growth.

Session 7: Caring Enough to Embrace Conflict

Why is there conflict in marriage?

What is the origin of marital conflict?

Let's review and discuss:

Notes

Read Genesis 3:1-16.

Genesis 3 (NIV)

The Fall

1 Now the serpent was more crafty than any of the wild animals the Lord God had made. He said to the woman, "Did God really say, 'You must not eat from any tree in the garden?'"

2 The woman said to the serpent, "We may eat fruit from the trees in the garden, 3 but God did say, 'You must not eat fruit from the tree that is in the middle of the garden, and you must not touch it, or you will die.'"

4 "You will not certainly die," the serpent said to the woman. 5 "For God knows that when you eat from it your eyes will be opened, and you will be like God, knowing good and evil."

6 When the woman saw that the fruit of the tree was good for food and pleasing to the eye, and also desirable for gaining wisdom, she took some and ate it. She also gave some to her husband, who was with her, and he ate it. 7 Then the eyes of both of them were opened, and they realized they were naked; so they sewed fig leaves together and made coverings for themselves.

8 Then the man and his wife heard the sound of the Lord God as he was walking in the garden in the cool of the day, and they hid from the Lord God among the trees of the garden. 9 But the Lord God called to the man, "Where are you?"

10 He answered, "I heard you in the garden, and I was afraid because I was naked; so I hid."

11 And he said, "Who told you that you were naked? Have you eaten from the tree that I commanded you not to eat from?"

12 The man said, "The woman you put here with me—she gave

me some fruit from the tree, and I ate it."

13 Then the Lord God said to the woman, "What is this you have done?"
The woman said, "The serpent deceived me, and I ate."

14 So the Lord God said to the serpent, "Because you have done this,
Cursed are you above all livestock
    and all wild animals!
You will crawl on your belly
    and you will eat dust
    all the days of your life.

15 And I will put enmity
    between you and the woman,
    and between your offspring and hers;
he will crush your head,
    and you will strike his heel."

16 To the woman he said,
"I will make your pains in childbearing very severe;
    with painful labor you will give birth to children.
Your desire will be for your husband,
    and he will rule over you."

Notes

The results of their sin were:

- Shame: Which verse depicts their shame?

- Guilt: What did they do as a result of their guilt?

- Fear: Where do we see the fear they had after their sin?

- Blame shifting: Focus on verses 11-14.

- CONFLICT: Read verses 15 and 16 again.

Session 7: Caring Enough to Embrace Conflict

The word "desire" in verse 16 is not a good thing. Gentlemen, this does not mean your wife will sexually desire you. In the middle of handing out punishment, God did not mix in good news for you. This is actually a curse, and it means that your wife will desire to "tell you what to do," desire to be the leader of the marriage.

Her desire will be to work against your position in the family and your response will be to "withdraw," "become silent," and by intentional actions or passive-aggressive actions, you will want to rule over her, rather than be the servant leader God intended you to be. Instead, after the fall, the marriage leadership of the man, as well as the inclinations of the woman, were perverted.

All this happened as a result of the fall. This is where marriage conflict began.

So marital conflict is a state produced by sin, and, of course, the architect of sin is Satan.

Keep in mind conflict is a spiritual attack, which we can only overcome using spiritual truths by embracing and having the mind of Christ.

You see, both Christian men and women have two natures:

1. Adam's sinful nature.
2. Christ's righteousness, which we can take on by trusting in Him.

The amount of conflict in a marriage will be governed by which man we emulate and which mind we have.

As we read on, we find Adam to be descriptive and Jesus the Son of Man to be prescriptive. Jesus is the one we watch, the one we worship, the one we ponder, and the one we praise.

Notes

One of the best poems I ever heard is, "Two natures beat within my chest. One is foul; the other is blessed. One I love; the other I hate, but the one I feed the most is the one that will dominate." I don't know where I heard it, however.

Remember:

- Conflict is a tactic Satan has orchestrated to destroy your marriage, but you don't have to fall victim to his evil intentions.

- Conflict is a spiritual battle.

- The result of sin is punishment in three ways:
    o Pain in work (Genesis 3:17-19)
    o Pain in childbirth (Genesis 3:16)
    o Pain in marriage relationships (Genesis 3:16)

Let's discuss how conflict helps us fulfill one of the purposes of marriage.

Marriage has three basic purposes:

1. **Procreation** – Genesis 1:28 – And God blessed them, and God said unto them, Be fruitful, and multiply, and replenish the earth, and subdue it: and have dominion over the fish of the sea, and over the fowl of the air, and over every living thing that moveth upon the earth.

2. **Sanctification** – The Greek word translated "sanctification" (*hagiasmos* [ajgiasmov]) means "holiness." To sanctify, therefore, means "to make holy."

3. **Divine Illustration** – Marriage is designed to be a God-centered relationship as well as a little piece of heaven here on earth. God designed marriage to mirror His relationship with the church, with Christ as the groom and servant leader, who gave His life for His bride – the church. The sacrifices Jesus made for His bride, together with His leadership style, teach us a lot about the different roles a man and a woman have in a marriage and how they should function in those roles. Also note that the divine Word of God begins with a wedding in

Session 7: Caring Enough to Embrace Conflict

Genesis 2:18-25 and ends with a wedding, Christ's return for the church, in Revelation 19:7-10.

Read Ephesians 5:21-33.

Do you see how this illustrates the type of relationship the marriage is to be?

- Orderly
- Sacrificial
- Responsible
- Satisfying

Sanctification is the purpose we want to concentrate on as we discuss conflict.

Your salvation and mine has three basic components. If you asked Jesus to save you in "Lose Your Mind If You Want To Love Your Spouse" then you've accomplished the first component: Justification.

Component # 1 is Justification. This basically means you have now been saved from the penalty of sin, which is death. Since Jesus has already died for us, we will never face that penalty even though we rightly deserve to. Does this make sense?

Component # 2 is Sanctification. In justification you were saved from the penalty of sin. In sanctification, you are being saved daily from the *power* of sin. In other words, every day I get a little better, and every day I become more and more like Jesus. The things I used to do I don't do anymore (or at least not as often), and sin loses its power over me as I decrease and Christ increases.

Component #3 is Glorification. Justification has saved me from the penalty of sin; Sanctification is saving me from the power of sin; and Glorification will save me from the very

Notes

presence of sin. That last one will happen when we go to spend eternity in heaven with our Father.

Now what does all this have to do with conflict? Well, I'm glad you asked.

God uses my spouse to sanctify me, and it is often done through conflict.

It's when Teresa has gotten on my last nerve and I decrease (respond to her like Christ does to me) so I can really grow.

That's how conflict leads to Sanctification.

1. Read James 4:1-12. According to this passage, why is there conflict?

_____

_____

_____

2. What does the passage say about people who are constantly engaged in conflict?

_____

_____

_____

3. What must be done to minimize conflict and restore order?

_____

_____

_____

4. In the midst of conflict, remember the goal is not to convince the other person that you are right. The goal is to determine, based on the Word of God, what is right.

Session 7: Caring Enough to Embrace Conflict

Three things not to do in the midst of conflict:

1. **Do not practice avoidance.** Care enough to confront. Some people avoid confrontation because they remember a time when they saw it escalate into a physical altercation.

2. **Do not practice appeasement.** One person always seems to win and the other always seems to lose. Compromise is okay; appeasement is not.

3. **Do not practice aggression.** Instead, speak the truth in love. A soft answer turns away wrath. There are few problems that husbands and wives can't solve if they attack the problem, not the person.

When you confront, chose the right time, use the right tone, and make sure it is on the right turf.

What does this statement mean to you?

_____

_____

_____

_____

_____

Three things to do to minimize conflict:

1. **Learn to accommodate.** Be willing to change yourself. By doing so, your spouse now has to react to something different.

2. **Learn to practice acceptance.** When I accommodate, I change. When I accept, I am willing to say my spouse may never change.

Notes

Getting married is like buying an old record. You buy it for what you want on one side, and you accept what you get on the other.

3. **Learn to make adjustments. We are different.** I am always willing to compromise on preferences but not principles.

What are some common subjects of conflict?

____ Finances

____ Friends

____ How we spend our time

____ Parents and in-laws

____ Career decisions

____ Children

____ Goals in life

____ Acceptable risks to take

____ Housing

____ How we make decisions

____ How we handle conflict – we even disagree about how we should disagree

____ Use of alcohol and drugs

____ Interest and activities

It's interesting how closely conflict and communication are related. Do you appreciate how much you could cut down on conflict if you just resolve these issues before you get married?

For most of our 29 years of marriage, Teresa was a stay-at-home mom. She worked like a dog caring for a husband and four children. Anyone who thinks a stay-at-home mom doesn't work has no idea what he or she is talking about.

Even though Teresa was under tremendous pressure from friends and family to "have a career" because she went to college just like I did, this was not a huge issue in our marriage. Why? Because we talked about it before we were married.

The entire purpose of this course is to allow you to go into marriage with your "eyes wide open," but how open your eyes are is based on how much you communicate.

Just like "If you don't communicate, your marriage will disintegrate," good communication works to lessen conflict and strengthen marriages!

Are you so interested in being right that you don't want to be bothered by the facts?

Remember James 4 – conflict is caused primarily by our selfishness. When conflict arises, follow this pattern:

1. Clearly define the problem.
2. Determine the biblical truths that speak to the problem.
3. Decide on practical ways to implement biblical truths in your situation.

Discuss a recent conflict with the group or group leader. Allow your group leader to walk you through the pattern just described to resolve the conflict. Remember, it's not about being right; it's about doing what is right.

Remember; it's okay to disagree, but you should never become disagreeable toward each other.

Explain what this statement means:

_____

_____

_____

_____

Notes

Additional Don'ts Involving Conflict

Don't condemn, don't criticize, and don't compare!

Read the two stories below:

1. One man said to his wife, "I can't believe God made you so beautiful and so dumb."

    The woman replied, "He made me beautiful so you would be attracted to me, and he made me dumb so I would be attracted to you."

2. One man said to his wife, "Why can't you cook biscuits like my momma used to?"

    The wife replied, "Why can't you bring home dough like my daddy did?"

What's wrong with the approach each of the couples is using in these stories?

_____

_____

_____

_____

_____

Session 7: Caring Enough to Embrace Conflict

Don't start a sentence with the word "you" in the midst of conflict.

"You" is an accusing sentence starter. "You" puts people on the defensive, and when they feel threatened, they may either lash out (attack) or retreat. Neither response helps resolve conflict.

Bad Example:
"You don't care about me. If you did, you wouldn't spend so much time at the gym with your friends."

Good Example:
"Honey, when I see the amount of time you spend at the gym with your friends, it makes me feel like you don't care about me."

See the difference? No one can dispute how you feel. A person might object what you say, how you say it, or when you said it, but you're the only one who can voice how you feel.

Don't dwell on the past.

One man said, "Every time we get in an argument, my wife gets historical."

His friend said, "You mean hysterical?"

"No," he said. "Every time we get in an argument, she brings up the past."

Notes

Off-limit responses in the midst of conflict:

- Using the words "never" or "always"
- Using negative words and making hurtful comments
- Bringing up the past
- Using bad language
- Threatening divorce

Add some of your own do's and don'ts to this list:

_____

_____

_____

How does your history affect how you disagree?

_____

_____

_____

Session 7: Caring Enough to Embrace Conflict

All of us enter relationships with baggage, or "stuff from our past," which determines how we respond in the present. If, for example, you grew up around yelling and screaming, and even physical altercations, you will more than likely want to handle conflict the same way in adulthood.

Again, this is why it is so important that you be "TRANSFORMED" – lose that old mind and put on the mind of Christ. Remember, what you saw, experienced, and learned growing up may have established a pattern you do or don't want to follow.

It's interesting to note that conflict resolution can't be separated from effective communication:

1. Be specific when you introduce an issue. Discuss only one issue at a time.

2. Don't simply complain; search for solutions and ask for reasonable change.

3. Consider compromise. Remember, your spouse's view of reality (based on his or her history and baggage) is as real to that person as yours is to you (based on your history and baggage.)

4. Never assume you know what others are thinking.

5. Never predict how he or she will react, or what he or she will accept or reject.

6. Don't overload your spouse with all your problems at once. That only makes him or her feel helpless and suggests you have been avoiding conflict by holding onto problems, and you have not been honest in speaking the truth in love at the appropriate time (read "sooner" rather than "later").

7. Never name-call or make "judgmental statements" about the other person.

8. Avoid taking "jabs."

9. Avoid using sarcasm as a weapon.

10. At all costs, avoid "going silent," even if the discussion is painful.

11. Avoid the phrases "you always" and "you never."

12. Use "I" messages and not "you" messages.

13. Deal with the conflict quickly. While it is acceptable to wait until one or both of you have cooled off, do not postpone the discussion indefinitely.

14. Don't try to win. The goal is to find a mutually satisfying solution where everyone wins.

 To listen to the podcast with Jim and Teresa discussing this session and additional resources, go to www.RelationshipSuccessUniversity.com/bookguide.

Session 8: Roles and Responsibilities: Being a Godly Husband and a Godly Wife

In no other place are unrealistic expectations and the effect of cultural influences more evident than in a discussion of the roles of husband and wife in a marriage.

Each of you has entered into this relationship with specific ideas about the roles you will play. These ideas have been formed by outside influences, such as how your mother played her role; how your father played his role; and what you hear from TV, talk shows, and other media.

Chances are you know very little about what God has said about the roles of husband and wife, or maybe you know what God has said, and you have misunderstood the meaning or disliked what you thought it meant and dismissed it.

Have you ever assembled something or cooked a new dish? Isn't it helpful if you follow the directions? Well, when Almighty God invented marriage, He laid out the instructions for a successful one.

We are going to examine what the original plan was, what went wrong with it, and how we operate today in an environment where the original plan has been distorted and demonized.

Our God is wonderful and loving. He has established a specific order (God is not a God of confusion and chaos), so when we read through the Word of God and we see where God has said "No," it is <u>not</u> to punish us. Actually, when God says "No," He is saying "Don't Hurt Yourself," and when He says, "Yes," He is saying, "Help Yourself."

God's plan and design for specific roles and a specific order in the home are not restrictive but liberating. Keep in mind that you (and to some extent, all of us) have been affected, influenced, trained, and conditioned by popular opinion. You can't hear a message over and over and not be affected and infected by that message (or else the price for a TV commercial during the 2015 Super Bowl wouldn't have been 4.5 million dollars for a 30-second spot). After all, what is a commercial but a message designed to get you to believe in and purchase the message or product being promoted?

During this session, we are going to start with the discussion questions, have some general discussion about how each of you views your roles in a marriage, split into groups of men and women to discuss your roles, and then come back together to share.

Remember, as we are discussing, the challenge is not necessarily to embrace what we have been taught (often in error), but to understand what God is teaching (He knows a thing or two about the roles since He invented them). His design is not antiquated, outdated, or wrong, no matter what you have been told.

Men: Outline what you believe to be your role in marriage and what you believe to be the role of your spouse:

_____

_____

_____

Women: Outline what you believe to be your role in marriage and what you believe to be the role of your spouse:

_____

_____

_____

Here are some specific discussion topics to help kickstart the process:

In this marriage, I see my role as:

_____

_____

In this marriage, I see the role of my spouse as:

_____

_____

Session 8: Roles and Responsibilities: Being a Godly Husband and a Godly Wife

When I hear that in marriage the husband is the head of the wife, I interpret that to mean:

_____

_____

When I hear the term "submit," I believe that means:

_____

_____

God created man and woman EQUAL, but not the same. Read Genesis 1:27.

What does "equal but not the same" mean?

_____

_____

Discuss "equal in value but different in function."

God created man and woman with the same values but different roles. God is a God of order and in His design of social order, God created man as the head. "Head" does not mean that he lords his male dominance over a woman and demands her total obedience to his every wish and command. God *never* viewed women as second-class citizens. His Word clearly states that we are all equally His children and are of equal value and worth before Him. As Galatians 3:28 tells us, "There is neither Jew nor Greek, slave nor free, male nor female, for you are all one in Christ Jesus."

Is there a difference between leadership and domination? Explain.

_____

_____

_____

What is a servant leader?

_____

_____

_____

_____

_____

_____

In his commentary on Ephesians, William Hendriksen points out that God:

> ...placed ultimate responsibility with respect to the household on the shoulders of the husband....The Lord has assigned the wife the duty of obeying her husband, yet...this obedience must be a voluntary submission on her part, and that only to her own husband, not to every man.

The New Testament clearly shows that men are to treat women with respect, reverence, and as equals. Unfortunately, many husbands have not received this message. Instead, they neglect their wives or treat them with insensitivity or abuse. One cause of the feminist movement may have been that men abandoned God's design.

When God presented Eve to Adam in the Garden, Adam received her as a gift of great value to God and to him. When husbands, particularly Christian husbands, do not treat their wives as precious gifts and helpmates from God, they can cause their wives to search for a way to find significance and value as people outside God's will.

Session 8: Roles and Responsibilities: Being a Godly Husband and a Godly Wife

Read Ephesians 5:22-33.

> 22 Wives, submit yourselves to your own husbands as you do to the Lord. 23 For the husband is the head of the wife as Christ is the head of the church, his body, of which he is the Savior. 24 Now as the church submits to Christ, so also wives should submit to their husbands in everything.
>
> 25 Husbands, love your wives, just as Christ loved the church and gave himself up for her 26 to make her holy, cleansing her by the washing with water through the word, 27 and to present her to himself as a radiant church, without stain or wrinkle or any other blemish, but holy and blameless.
>
> 28 In this same way, husbands ought to love their wives as their own bodies. He who loves his wife loves himself. 29 After all, no one ever hated their own body, but they feed and care for their body, just as Christ does the church— 30 for we are members of his body. 31 "For this reason a man will leave his father and mother and be united to his wife, and the two will become one flesh." 32 This is a profound mystery—but I am talking about Christ and the church.
>
> 33 However, each one of you also must love his wife as he loves himself, and the wife must respect her husband.

SUBMISSION. I put this in all caps not because I'm screaming at you, but because I want to tackle this issue head on. Today, if you ask ten women what they think of the term "submission," eleven would respond that it is a negative term.

What does the Bible say submission means? I'm so glad you asked. This gives us a chance to share God's definition, not anyone else's.

The Greek word for submission (this is important because this passage was written in Greek and later translated into English) is *hupotasso*, which means "to place or arrange under." Submission is not blind obedience; neither is it silent suffering. Instead the word defines a voluntary subordination to a recognized authority, in this case the divinely appointed authority of the husband.

Notes

Notes

God asks the woman to voluntarily place herself under the authority of the man.

Like it, don't like it, there has to be a sense of order and responsibility. Even in something as simple as dancing, someone has to take the lead.

Below are examples of people you submit to daily:

- Employers
- Police officers
- Coaches

So submission is not a foreign or demeaning term in and of itself, but many men and women have allowed culture to define the term instead of understanding what the term actually

> "During the last few decades our culture has redefined the meaning and responsibilities of man and woman in society and in the home. Many men are confused and insecure. Many do not know how to act in the home. Growing up, they lacked a good model for leadership at home and have no mental picture of what it means to lead a family. Consequently, they do not lead effectively, or they do not even try.
>
> Increasingly, many men are becoming passive in the home. They have decided that the easiest thing to do is nothing. The simplest thing—with the smallest risk—is to stay on the fence with both feet firmly planted in mid-air and let the wife do it. When a man is married to a strong wife who will take over, he often lets her do just that.
>
> Fortunately, there is an answer. The Scriptures clearly give us the model for being a man, a husband, and father. I call that model the 'servant/leader.'"
>
> -- Dennis Rainey

means. Think of the lead officer with a battalion of men in battle formation.

The term *hupotasso* or "submit" was used by a commander telling his soldiers to arrange themselves as instructed. The commanding officer is not "better" or of "more value" than the officers under his "authority"; to have order, however, there has to be a leader and Almighty God has declared that to be the husband.

Tony Evans defined submitting as "ducking so God can hit your husband."

Although the wife is responsible for her submission, it is the husband's responsibility to lead in such a way that makes following him reasonable and enjoyable for her.

Why is submission important?

_____

_____

_____

Because marriage is much like a "relational dance," the question most couples struggle with is, "Who is leading and who is following"? God answered that question when He invented marriage.

When scripture calls the woman the man's helper, what do you think that means?

_____

_____

_____

Read Genesis 2:18-20.

> 18 The LORD God said, "It is not good for the man to be alone. I will make a helper suitable for him."
>
> 19 Now the LORD God had formed out of the ground all the wild animals and all the birds in the sky. He brought them to the man to see what he would name them; and whatever the man called each living creature, that was its name. 20 So the man gave names to all the livestock, the birds in the sky and all the wild animals. But for Adam no suitable helper was found.

Scripture is clear that first and foremost, wives are called to be helpers for their husbands. Even though our society has made "helper" a demeaning term, it is certainly not in God's eyes.

The word "helper" is used 3 other times in scripture, in addition to being used to describe a woman's marital role. The three other times refer to God the Father, God the Son, and God the Holy Spirit. Obviously then, "helper" is not a demeaning term. The woman as "helper" is to complement the man rather than to compete with him!

Your wife is to be your completer, not your competitor!

Session 8: Roles and Responsibilities: Being a Godly Husband and a Godly Wife

Man as the Head of the Family

Once again, the reason we struggle with this idea is because today's culture has demonized it. Remember, today's culture teaches that to be equal means to be the same. Men and women are equal (in value) but not the same (in function).

What are your thoughts on equality and value?

_____

_____

_____

Let's discuss how and why culture has disengaged from the Word of God.

Read 1 Corinthians 11:3.

> 3 But I want you to realize that the head of every man is Christ, and the head of the woman is man, and the head of Christ is God.

Is Jesus Christ equal to God in value and deity? Discuss:

_____

_____

_____

Read John 5:18.

> "For this reason they tried all the more to kill him; not only was he breaking the Sabbath, but he was even calling God his own Father, making himself equal with God."

Notes

Now read John 14:5-14.

> 5 Thomas said to him, "Lord, we don't know where you are going, so how can we know the way?"
>
> 6 Jesus answered, "I am the way and the truth and the life. No one comes to the Father except through me. 7 If you really know me, you will know my Father as well. From *now* on, you do know him and have seen him."
>
> 8 Philip said, "Lord, show us the Father and that will be enough for us."
>
> 9 Jesus answered: "Don't you know me, Philip, even after I have been among you such a long time? Anyone who has seen me has seen the Father. How can you say, 'Show us the Father'? 10 Don't you believe that I am in the Father, and that the Father is in me? The words I say to you I do not speak on my own authority. Rather, it is the Father, living in me, who is doing his work.
>
> 11 Believe me when I say that I am in the Father and the Father is in me; or at least believe on the evidence of the works themselves. 12 Very truly I tell you, whoever believes in me will do the works I have been doing, and they will do even greater things than these, because I am going to the Father. 13 And I will do whatever you ask in my name, so that the Father may be glorified in the Son. 14 You may ask me for anything in my name, and I will do it.

Read Philippians 2:5-7.

> 5 In your relationships with one another, have the same mindset as Christ Jesus:
>
> 6 Who, being in very nature God, did not consider equality with God something to be used to his own advantage; 7 rather, he made himself nothing by taking the very nature of a servant....

The answer to the question is a resounding YES!

Is Christ the same as God in position and function? Discuss:

_____

_____

_____

_____

Read Matthew 26:39.

> 39 Going a little farther, he fell with his face to the ground and prayed, "My Father, if it is possible, may this cup be taken from me. Yet not as I will, but as you will."

A great example of Jesus Christ submitting to (placing Himself under the authority of) the will of the Father is in this verse. The human side of Christ (remember when Jesus came to earth, He took on the form of a man) would have preferred not to go through the ordeal of being nailed to and hung on a cross until He died (crucifixion), but even with the horrendous death facing Him, Jesus recognized the position of God the Father and subjected Himself to God the Father's will.

So when it comes to equality, value, and self-worth being at odds with headship and submission, case closed.

So the answer to the question, "Is Christ the same as God in position and function?" the answer is a resounding NO!

"Ok, Teresa and Jim, if this is the case, what went wrong and why is it so hard to apply all this in our marriages today?" Great question and I'm glad you asked.

At creation, everything was good. God assigned the roles of

men and women in a marriage before the fall when male leadership was noble, honorable, and as far as women were concerned, it was personally gratifying, not terrifying.

After the fall, everything changed! We discussed this in a previous chapter, but here we want to bring out some different applications of the Genesis 3 passage. This is really important!

Let's discuss a few questions first.

When sin entered the world through the serpent (Satan) in the Garden…

Where was Adam while Eve was talking with Satan? (off working, watching TV, at the mall)?

_____

_____

_____

_____

_____

Who was the first person to eat the forbidden fruit?

_____

Who did God hold primarily responsible for the sin?

_____

Let's match your answers with scripture.

Session 8: Roles and Responsibilities: Being a Godly Husband and a Godly Wife

Genesis 3 (NIV) The Fall

1 Now the serpent was more crafty than any of the wild animals the LORD God had made. He said to the woman, "Did God really say, 'You must not eat from any tree in the garden'?"

2 The woman said to the serpent, "We may eat fruit from the trees in the garden, 3 but God did say, 'You must not eat fruit from the tree that is in the middle of the garden, and you must not touch it, or you will die.'"

4 "You will not certainly die," the serpent said to the woman. 5 "For God knows that when you eat from it your eyes will be opened, and you will be like God, knowing good and evil."

6 When the woman saw that the fruit of the tree was good for <u>food</u> and pleasing to the eye, and also desirable for gaining wisdom, she took some and ate it. She also gave some to her husband, who was with her, and he ate it. 7 Then the eyes of both of them were opened, and they realized they were naked; so they sewed fig leaves together and made coverings for themselves.

8 Then the man and his wife heard the sound of the LORD God as he was walking in the garden in the cool of the day, and they hid from the LORD God among the trees of the garden. 9 But the LORD God called to the man, "Where are you?"

10 He answered, "I heard you in the garden, and I was afraid because I was naked; so I hid."

11 And he said, "Who told you that you were naked? Have you eaten from the tree that I commanded you not to eat from?"

12 The man said, "The woman you put here with me—she gave me some fruit from the tree, and I ate it."

13 Then the LORD God said to the woman, "What is this you have done?"

The woman said, "The serpent deceived me, and I ate."

Notes

After the fall, everything changed. Now the woman, a sinner, would be married to a big "sinner" and give birth to little "sinners."

Read Genesis 3:14-16.

> 14 So the LORD God said to the serpent, "Because you have done this, "Cursed are you above all livestock and all wild animals! You will crawl on your belly and you will eat dust all the days of your life. 15 And I will put enmity between you and the woman, and between your offspring and hers; he will crush your head, and you will strike his heel." 16 To the woman he said, "I will make your pains in childbearing very severe; with painful labor you will give birth to children. Your desire will be for your husband, and he will rule over you."

Pay special attention to the last part of verse 16!

The punishment because of the fall did not dictate the roles of men and women in a marriage; it simply complicated the already-existing roles.

Notice that Adam's sin unleashed the clash of female disobedience and the destructive curse of male domination in Genesis 3:6b – "Your 'desire' shall be for your husband, and he shall rule over you." This has nothing to do with your wife physically desiring you. This is not a good thing!

See Genesis 4:7.

The "fall" or "curse" unleashes the woman's rebellion to the headship of man, and instead of leading, man now has a "bent" to dominate. The woman's desire will be to usurp her husband's authority or position. Because of the fall and subsequent curse, husband and wife will clash over control. Even in the midst of the clash, however, the God-ordained order will not be dismissed. The husband will still remain in authority and rule over his wife, albeit in a fallen sense, not as God originally designed. The fall "perverted" God's original design.

This perversion, however, does not change the original design. Wives should not desire their husbands' position and husbands should not rule harshly. Stick to the original plan. How do you do that? In Christ – the second Adam! Only when you lose your mind can you love each other like God intended. (See Session 4: "Lose Your Mind and Love Your Spouse").

As a result of the fall, man no longer leads easily; he must fight for his headship. Sin has corrupted both the willing submission of the wife and the loving headship of the husband. As a result, the rule of love founded in paradise is replaced by struggle, tyranny, and domination. The "desire" of the woman in Genesis 3:16b does not make her more submissive to her husband so that he may rule over her. Her desire is to contend with him for leadership in their relationship. This desire is a result of, and a just punishment for, sin, but it is not God's original will for the wife.

Thus, God is saying a woman's desire will be to gain the upper hand over her husband, but because she is the "weaker vessel" (1 Peter 3:7), her husband will put her down by force if need be. The curse is that women will lose the battle of the sexes. History bears this out.

Until the advent of women's rights movements, women were virtually their husband's property, treated as heir-producing machines, given little freedom, and forced to serve their husbands' every whim. In many cultures, men bought and sold women like cattle. Some cultures maintain this custom even today.

Only where true Christianity flourishes is there any real easing of this curse. Ephesians 5:22-33 teaches how we can decrease its effects within our marriages—by emulating the virtues of Christ's relationship with the church. Thus, wives are told to submit rather than contend, and husbands are commanded to love rather than dominate. It takes a conscious effort to overcome the evil, ingrained habits of 6,000 years of misguided practice.

Notes

Do you remember when we said in an earlier session that the purpose of marriage was threefold?

Procreation, Sanctification, and Illustration

This is the illustration part. Just as Jesus and God are one, Genesis 2:24 calls us to be one in our marriages.

Just as there is order with God the Father and God the Son, God designed marriage as an institution with a specific order and specific roles for husbands and wives.

And, just as there is obedience between the Son and the Father, there is to be obedience in marriage. Women are to choose to submit to their husbands' leadership with respect, according to Titus 2:5 and 1 Peter 3:1-4. 1 Peter 3:1-4 states that when wives submit to their husbands' leadership, they are doing it as service to God.

Husbands are to follow God's instruction and Christ's example to be servant leaders, not passive as Adam was in Genesis 3:6, and not domineering as men tend to be. Rather, they are to lead as a service unto God. So what happens in a marriage? Three become one.

A great marriage is only great if the husband is submitting to the leadership of God and the wife is submitting to the leadership of the husband so that there is a submitted husband, a submitted wife, and a Supreme God! Men and women were created with distinct abilities to fulfill these biblical roles, and when husbands and wives follow the biblical pattern within the home, they bring glory to God as a picture of Christ and His church, thus the illustration.

Session 8: Roles and Responsibilities: Being a Godly Husband and a Godly Wife

A Helpful Resource on the Biblical Roles from *Maranatha Life* by Deborah Murphy

THE BELIEVING WIFE

1. **Sex** – Sexual Intimacy/One Flesh <u>Relationship</u> – 1 Corinthians 7:2-5; Ephesians 5:31; Genesis 2:24-25.

    - Without sex, a couple co-exists as roommates, not lovers.
    - Leaves her father and her mother.
    - Sexually pleases her husband – 1 Corinthians 7:33.
    - <u>Meditates</u> sexually on her husband – Song of Solomon 5:10-16; Song of Solomon 7:10.
    - Desires him, responds sexually to him without embarrassment.

2. **Submission** – <u>Submits</u> to his authority and leadership as her covering, with heartfelt obedience.

    - In everything – not only in what she chooses – Ephesians 5:24.
    - As to the Lord – Ephesians 5:21; Colossians 3:18.
    - Rebellion toward <u>her</u> husband is equal to rebellion against God who gave him the responsibility to be her covering.
    - <u>Demonstrates</u> her love through obedience from her heart.
    - Remains under his "covering of authority" by submitting to him.
    - Accepts and responds to his <u>evaluations</u> and his correction.
    - Is responsible toward her husband.
    - Does not dominate, manipulate, control, boss, scold, nag, or argue... against his delegated God-given authority.

Notes

3. **Reverence** – Gives respect and honor to her husband – Ephesians 5:33.

- Does him good and not evil all the days of her life – Proverbs 31:11-12.
- Honors him by accepting his leadership.
- Uses words that honor him, not insult or depreciate him.
- Listens attentively to him, and remembers what he said. It is important because he said it.
- Makes his priorities her priorities.
- Doesn't speak negatively about him to <u>family members</u>, friends, or people at church.
- Asks for and values his opinions.

4. **Godly behavior** – Chaste and respectful speech – 1 Peter 3:1-6.

- Uses words that are helpful, and without reproach, along with good behavior – Titus 2:3-5.
- Always rejoices in the Lord, and in the husband that he gave her.
- Is not fearful of anything or anyone – (this is mentioned in the Bible more than 365 times).
- Thinks on things that are good, true, and holy – Philippians 4:8.
- Does not gossip or complain.
- Avoids sinning.

5. **Support** – A helpmeet – Genesis 2:18

- "Helpmeet" is a technical word used in the <u>construction</u> of buildings. It's the substance added around a column to strengthen it so it can support additional weight or stress.
- Strengthens him by praising and thanking him for what he does for her.
- Encourages him through her actions and her words.
- Upholds him in ways that show her confidence in him.
- Raises her husband's self-esteem by delighting to spend time with him.

Session 8: Roles and Responsibilities: Being a Godly Husband and a Godly Wife

- Surrounds him with her haceed love – with all her being: body, emotions, mind, and spirit.
- Fulfills well her other responsibilities in the <u>home</u> (children, kitchen, housework, etc.)

THE BELIEVING HUSBAND

1. **Sex** – Nurture their sexual relationship/Their Oneness – 1 Corinthians 7:2-5; Ephesians 5:31; Genesis 2:24.

    - Leaves his father and mother.
    - Enjoys and rejoices with his wife's body – Proverbs 5:15-19.
    - Pleases his wife – 1 Corinthians 7:33.
    - Consoles (emotionally comforts) his wife by lovemaking.– 2 Samuel 12:24.
    - Maintains the frequency and passion within their sexual relationship.
    - Protect them both from sexual temptations.
    - Faithfulness/fidelity to her in both his thoughts and his actions.
    - Values and cherishes sexual intimacy with his wife.
    - Priorities – God is #1; wife is #2; then come children, ministry, and secular <u>work</u>.

2. **Headship/Covering/Leadership/Authority** delegated by God – Ephesians 5:23-24

    - Sets aside his own wisdom in order to use God's wisdom.
    - Is a responsible husband – passivity is sin.
    - Teaches his wife to be submitted in her actions, reactions, and choices she makes.
    - Takes the responsibility and right to instruct and correct her.
    - Provides positive and negative consequences.
    - Doesn't tolerate rebellion, manipulation, and control against his authority.

Notes

3. **Haceed Love** – Loves her with Haceed/Agape Love – Ephesians 5:25-33

    - Helps her grow and mature in her walk with the Lord/teaches her His Word.
    - Is not bitter toward her, forgives her – Colossians 3:19.
    - Is her best friend and lover.
    - Motivates her to become more Godly.
    - Has daily chats with her about issues before they can become large problems. Deals with these things – doesn't passively ignore them.
    - Encourages her, praises her.

4. **Honor** – Gives honor to her, asks God for wisdom to understand her, prays with her – 1 Peter 3:7

    - Respects her as a gift and a treasure from God.
    - Doesn't look sexually at other women.
    - Uses good words toward her in agreement with the Bible.
    - Asks for her opinions, ideas, and thoughts.

5. **Provides for her and your children** (financially, emotionally, and spiritually)

    - Is the priest within his home – 1 Timothy 5:8.
    - Is responsible for her and the children.
    - Knows that what she wants is not always what she needs.
    - Allows her to talk with you, and listens attentively to her. She needs to share her feelings with you – not bottle them up.
    - Provides whatever is needed in order to attend church services and activities, along with Christian fellowship with other believers.
    - Initiates prayer and Bible study in his home.
    - Protects.

To listen to the podcast with Jim and Teresa discussing this session and additional resources, go to www.RelationshipSuccessUniversity.com/bookguide.

Session 9: The Money

Money is the topic most written about in the Bible. In fact, there are more than 2,300 verses dedicated to financial mindsets and decisions. God teaches us that how we handle money reflects our faith in Him. He often uses our financial circumstances to draw us closer to Him as He guides us.

Years ago I decided I wanted to know more about how to manage money in our marriage. So I went to a training seminar in Memphis, Tennessee, sponsored by Larry Burkett of Christian Financial Concepts. The training helped me so much that I became a Certified Instructor and started a small group at church that taught what the Bible says about money.

Teresa and I were clueless. We literally started the process by writing on a yellow pad (that was before smart phones and apps) for 30 days every penny we spent and assigning categories to those pennies so we could see where our money was being spent.

Once we had this information, we could more intelligently construct a plan for spending money in our marriage. This spending plan is called a *budget*!

In our experience, we have seen money cause huge problems in marriages. The sad thing is these problems could certainly be reduced and probably eliminated if couples just took the time and developed a plan for the money.

Our family will be forever grateful for the training we received at the feet of Larry Burkett and Christian Financial Concepts (now Crown Financial Ministries).

> "Money is an outside indicator of an inward spiritual condition."
>
> — Larry Burkett
> Cofounder of Crown Money Map

The Word of God has given clear, solid principles and guidelines for handling finances and answers such questions as:

- What is God's plan for family finances?
- What should our attitudes be about money?
- How does God want us to handle money?

If at all possible, look for or ask about starting a money management ministry at your church.

The money management principles we learned helped build such a strong foundation that even when we faced financial ruin, we remained relationship rich.

We used our life savings, about $250,000, as a down payment on a block of 70 rental homes left to an estate. The remaining purchase price, $1,250,000, was owner financed. Over the next 6 years, we bought and sold about 300 homes and apartment buildings, we grew to a staff of 20 employees, and we had one of the largest residential real estate investment firms in the Southeast. Inside our office operation was a real estate agency, a mortgage company, a property management company, a private lending institution, as well as landscaping and property renovation services. We were a one-stop shop for all things real estate. This was going to be our family business. In fact, our two oldest children were working in the business while attending school.

We were blowing and going, literally real estate millionaires, when we lost everything in the real estate market crash of the mid-2000s. Our personal dream home on seven acres of land with a tennis court, walking trail, and fruit orchard were all foreclosed upon. This was a home we were scheduled to pay for in 12 years, rather than the traditional 30. But in the midst of it all, our marriage grew stronger and stronger. That's the upside of getting this part of your relationship right.

Session 9: The Money

If we can survive this kind of disaster and remain relationship rich in the face of financial ruin, so can you.

Let's see where you are. Discuss your personal views on the following:

a. Joint or separate bank accounts
b. Who will pay the bills and handle day-to-day financial matters?
c. Giving to the church and to family members
d. Wife working outside the home
e. Savings, investments, and risks
f. Cooking vs. going out to dinner
g. Having a written plan for our finances (a budget)
h. Life insurance and a will
i. As a family, how will you make decisions about purchases?
j. What place does credit have in this family?
k. Are you a spender or a saver?

Chances are most of the attitude you have about money came from what you observed when you were growing up in your parents' home. Maybe you are following the pattern of your parents or maybe what you saw at home was so unappealing, it has driven you to manage money completely opposite of the way they did it. Your mom or dad, for example, may have been so restrictive about money that you are now are a really big spender or vice versa.

Notes

Remember our discussion about the "baggage" we bring into a relationship?

Let's discuss what you saw when you were growing up:
- Did you parents discuss money with you?
- Were they savers or spenders?
- Were they generous givers?
- Did they make joint decisions about money?
- Did they buy new or used cars?
- Did they pay bills on time or were their creditors constantly hassling them?
- Who was in charge of the finances?
- Were your parents self-employed or employees?
- Discuss how each of your respective parents differed on his or her views of finances.

What are some mistakes you see people make in handling their finances?

___

___

___

Now let's see how the Word of God compares with what people think:

- Is the money actually yours? Read Psalm 24:1.
- When you deposit money in the bank, does that money then belong to the branch manager?
- How would you define stewardship?
  Biblical Passages on Faithful Stewardship
    ☐ Matthew 24:45-51; Luke 12:42-48 The Faithful and Wise Servant
    ☐ Matthew 25:14-30; Luke 19:11-27 The Talents/The Minas
    ☐ Mark 13:34-37 The Watchful Servants

How should an understanding of biblical stewardship shape the way we view our material possessions and finances? How should this play out in a marriage?

___

___

Session 9: The Money

> "[Stewardship] is taking God's resources—which is time, talent, treasures, relationships, influence—and using it for His purposes because everything I have has come from Him."
> — Ron Blue

What does the Bible say about how we give? Read Malachi 3:7-12

_____

_____

_____

Where do riches and abundance come from? Read 1 Chronicles 29:11-12, 14-16

_____

_____

_____

How would you respond to the following statement? God is only concerned about the tithe (10%), after I give that, I can do what I please with the rest of my money:

_____

_____

_____

Based on your background (your baggage) are you anxious about your family's finances?

_____ Yes _____ No

Read Matthew: 6:25-33. Embracing this passage will make it so much easier for you to turn over you money anxieties to God.

Remember Genesis 2:24?

- There is no more mine, only ours.
- Don't keep secrets about money from your spouse.
- Work together as a team.
- Set goals together.
- Develop your spending plan (budget) together.
- Discuss and make decisions together.
- Remember money is a spiritual indicator; our financial decisions are spiritual decisions.

Do you reconcile your checkbook? Why? Why not?

_____

_____

_____

_____

_____

Do you have a financial management system/app/program?

____ Yes ____ No

Remember the yellow legal pad? There are better tools here in the 21st century to help you achieve the same results. We encourage you to visit Crown Financial Ministries at www.crown.org for everything you need to become proficient with your money.

Jim and I interviewed a wonderful couple with a ministry concentrating specifically on money in relationships. Tai and Talaat at HisandHerMoney.com are a great resource.

We asked them to share a tidbit of info that we could include in this resource and their story and their contribution is below. His and Her Money is a journey of how two high school sweethearts fell in love, got married, but were total opposites when it came to handling their finances.

1. One had debt and the other did not.
2. One made poor money decisions while the other made better money decisions.
3. One had a low credit score and the other had a stellar credit score.

We had some very serious issues that we had to face when we made the decision to unite our marriage…

- Do we let our credit scores dictate if we are compatible for marriage?
- How will our previous money habits play a role in our marriage?
- Do we merge our finances together?
- How can we work together to become better at life and win with money?
- Is there any hope for our future?
- What does it feel like when one spouse has zero debt to now having $30,000 in debt?
- Am I a loser because I have now made my debt problems my future spouse's problems?
- Can I change or is my past really who I am?
- Should I have a secret account just in case our money situation gets worse?
- How will we purchase a home? Do we put it in both of our names and risk having a low interest rate due to the lower credit score?
- Do I have to take full responsibility for our finances simply because I'm better at it?
- When do we start to expand our family?
- Will we have to rely on two incomes to run our home?
- What will our lives look like 5 years from now?

Notes

These are all real questions that we asked ourselves before we said "I Do". With this resource we invite you into our home and personal lives. We will show you just how we climbed our way out of the debt trap not once, but TWICE…TOGETHER. It was not always pretty and glamorous. But, by God's grace and guidance, we are winning and becoming better stewards over our finances every day.

The first place you should begin, is by learning how to dream together. The truth of the matter is that you will not be able to effectively begin to turn things around financially, unless you have a clear picture of where you are trying to get to. By sitting down and dreaming together, you are both collectively engaging in seeing what life would be like if your finances were in order.

It is extremely important that you create solid financial goals with one another. Creating goals together, will help you to continue to support each other in the accomplishment of your dreams. There is no greater support that you can have, than that of the person that you have pledged your everlasting love to. In order for you both to adequately support each other, you each need to both have a clear picture of the goals that you want to achieve.

A goal setting tip that is an absolute must is to write your goals down. A goal that is not written down, is just simply an idea. The Bible also supports this conviction, in Habakkuk 2:2 which states:

… Write the vision, and make it plain…

It's not good enough just to write your goals down any sort of way. As you are writing down your financial goals, you need to make sure that you are writing them down in the S.M.A.R.T. format. When we say SMART goals, we are not speaking about a level of intelligence by any means. We're simply saying that your goals should be Specific, Measurable, Attainable, Relevant, and Time-bound.

For starters, your financial goals must be very specific. When you make your goals specific, they depict to you exactly what is expected as an end result of the goal. It's not good enough to simply set a goal of, "I plan to get out of debt". That is way too vague of a goal. Instead, be more specific and say, "I plan to eliminate my $15,000 student loan that I owe to Sallie Mae, within the next 18 months". By making your goal specific, you can easily measure your progress toward its' completion.

If your financial goals are not measurable, you will never know whether you're making progress toward successfully accomplishing it. What's more, it will become difficult for you to stay disciplined or encouraged to complete your goals, when they have no milestones to indicate their progress. So, if you have a goal to increase your net worth by $30,000 within the next 24 months, break that number down into $2,000 milestones to track your progress.

Your personal finance goals must be something that is realistically attainable for you to reach. The best goals will require you to stretch out to achieve them, but they shouldn't require a miracle from on high for you to reach them either. That is, the goals are neither out of reach, nor to easy to attain. For instance, if your income is $40,000 annually, then it would not be a good idea to set a goal to pay off your $100,000 mortgage in the next 6 months. That is not truly a realistic goal, based on your current financial situation. On the flip side, if you have an annual income of $85,000, don't set a goal of paying off a $500 credit card balance over the next 12 months. Goals that are set too high or too low become meaningless, and you will naturally begin to ignore them.

Your goals must be relevant to your desired financial destination, in the short and long term. When it comes to your household financial picture, where would you like to be 6 to 12 months from now? Moreover, what do you want your financial picture to look like, 5 to 10 years from now? Assemble all of your financial goals with these benchmarks in mind.

Notes

Lastly, each of your financial goals must have starting points, ending points, to be considered time-bound. Incorporating deadlines into your goals will help you focus all of your efforts on completing the goal, on or before its due date. Financial goals without deadlines, tend to be overtaken by the day-to-day issues of life, that will invariably arise.

To listen to the podcast with Jim and Teresa discussing this session and additional resources, go to www.RelationshipSuccessUniversity.com/bookguide.

Session 10: Sanctified, Satisfying, and Sizzling Married Sex!

Genesis 1
27 God created mankind in his own image, in the image of God he created them; male and female he created them. 28 God blessed them and said to them, "Be fruitful and increase in number; fill the earth and subdue it. Rule over the fish in the sea and the birds in the sky and over every living creature that moves on the ground." … 31 God saw all that he had made, and it was very good. And there was evening, and there was morning—the sixth day.

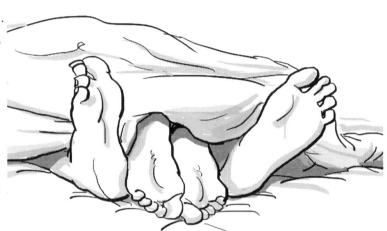

There it is, right there in the Word of God – the invention of sex. God actually *commanded* the man and woman to have sex with one another. They would have been disobedient if they didn't have sex. God created sex…and it was good!

Let me ask you a question. Is there anything wrong with fire? My answer is, "It depends."

Fire in the fireplace warms. It's pleasant to look at, and it brightens the environment of the entire home. But a fire in the middle of your family room floor can burn the whole house down. Fire has a proper place. In its right place, it is good. In the wrong place, it's dangerous. So it is with sex.

Sex outside of marriage is dangerous and directly against the Word of God. Sex in a marriage is good and exactly as God intended. So let it burn!

We have counseled people in poor marriages who still have sex, and we have counseled people in poor marriages who no longer have sex, but we have never counseled a kind, loving, compassionate, couple engaged in a great marriage not having great sex (outside of some medical issue).

Great sex is the culmination of everything we have discussed. Rarely will there be a couple who has great communication skills and excellent conflict resolution skills, but a poor sex life.

For women, sex is very much an emotional act. With men it is usually more physical. Sex, within the confines of the marriage, is one of the greatest gifts God has given men and women. Our culture today has perverted that wonderful gift. Sex in the wrong place and at the wrong time (before marriage) has actually made most people uncomfortable discussing it.

Here is where things went wrong:

> Genesis 2:25: Adam and his wife were both naked, and they felt no shame.

> Genesis 3:7: Then the eyes of both of them were opened, and they realized they were naked; so they sewed fig leaves together and made coverings for themselves.

In Genesis 2:25, both the man and the woman were naked and not ashamed. This speaks to more than just their nakedness. They were able to bare their most intimate feelings before each other in addition to being comfortable naked.

In Genesis 3:7, sin distorts the original plan. Today, for the most part, we are no longer genuinely open and honest with each other for fear of being hurt, and many are unable to completely enjoy sex as God intended because of their lack of comfort with their own bodies.

"I need to lose some weight"; "I wish my hips were smaller"; "I wish my breasts were bigger"; I wish my waist was smaller"; and the list goes on and on. Basically we are no longer naked and not ashamed, and this greatly affects many couples' enjoyment of sex.

Session 10: Sanctified, Satisfying, and Sizzling Married Sex!

Are the following statements True or False? Place a T or F next to each statement and discuss your answers.

a. ____ Married couples should freely discuss sex, what pleases them, likes, and dislikes.

b. ____ Women should not initiate sex with their husbands.

c. ____ Men enjoy sex more than women.

d. ____ It is okay to withhold sex to teach your spouse a lesson.

e. ____ Sex is about your own personal satisfaction.

f. ____ It is okay to demand sex.

g. ____ Sex makes a great bargaining tool.

h. ____ God is pleased with marital sex.

i. ____ Sexual problems and issues are often the result of past sexual histories and personal issues.

j. ____ Sexual fantasies about your spouse are not to be encouraged.

k. ____ Since marital sex is a private and personal matter, any problems should not be discussed with anyone other than your spouse.

l. ____ Whatever is mutually enjoyable and gratifying to the couple and does not hurt anyone or violate Biblical principles is proper in the confines of your bedroom.

m. ____ While most men experience an orgasm during sex, it is normal for a woman not to experience an orgasm.

n. ____ Sex should only happen in the dark and in silence.

o. ____ While engaged in sex, your primary purpose is to please your spouse.

Notes

Discussion Questions

1. What embarrasses you about sex?

2. If you engaged in sex prior to marriage, how are you going to move past the reluctance and feelings of guilt you may have so you can feel completely free to have sex within the confines of your marriage?

3. In an effort to keep sex from their children, many parents demean or "dirty" sex. What did your parents tell you about sex, and as a result, what are your attitudes?

4. As you approach marriage, what are your thoughts about sex? Your concerns? Your expectations?

5. Do you understand the differences between men and women when it comes to sex? What are some of the differences?

6. What thoughts or actions make you feel guilty or ashamed about sex?

7. How often should a couple have sex?

8. What should couples do if they are experiencing problems in this area of their marriage?

9. What are your birth control plans?

The sexual differences between men and women are a whole lot more than physiological. I am a big fan of Robert Lewis. Every man in America should read his book *Raising a Modern Day Knight*. Every week I lead a group of men in manhood training. Much of what I teach is taken from the works fo Robert Lewis. Lewis, the founder of www.MensFraternity.com and www.AuthenticManhood.com, teaches in his *Winning at Work and at Home* series, the following information as it relates to Man and Woman's Sexuality.

SEX

- On average how many times does a woman think about sex a day?

- On average how many times does a man think about sex a day?

- The best married couples having the best sex don't guess about sex- they communicate!

- Taken from Iron Men Session on Improving Your Sex Life

A Man's Sexuality: What Men Wish Their Wives Knew

Research has demonstrated that men are wired to desire sex, think about sex, and want to have sex. The average man wants sex two to three times a week, but of course that number will vary with a man's age and physical condition. Without sex, research shows, a man begins to feel tense, uncomfortable, uneasy, and often angry, even in his relationship with his wife.

Interestingly enough, this is similar to the way a woman feels when there is something undone in the home or not right in the relationship.

Men need sex! It's the way men were created and that is good! This is something a lot of wives do not understand. Proverbs 14:1 says, "The wise woman builds her house, but with her own hands the foolish one tears hers down." A wife untrained in the area of a man's desire for sex can literally tear her own house down.

A man must learn to manage his sexuality, however. Lewis teaches that when a man fails to properly manage sex, it becomes a WMD – weapon of mass destruction. This can lead to betrayal, disrespect, embarrassment, loss of honor, loss of reputation, loss of family, spreading of disease, and loss of job.

In other words, in one single moment, everything he has worked for can be gone.

On the other hand, when a man properly manages sex, it becomes a WMG – wonderful masculine gift. Sex properly focused, sex properly directed, is a wonderful gift from God.

So how does a man refrain from becoming a slave to his sexuality?

Wives, understand that your husband's sex drive is potent, powerful, persistent, and...normal.

Sex to him is what affection is to you (affection is the #1 need of most women). Sex for him is an escape from the reality of normal everyday life. It's a place where a husband can experience pure fun.

Sex reaffirms a man in his manhood and sexual fulfillment for men is impossible unless I can sexually fulfill you.

There are five basic stages of sex, though men and women experience and respond to these stages very differently.

- **Stage 1 – Love making.** It's the little things you do and say.

- **Stage 2 – Arousal.** The physical act of starting to put together the emotional act from Stage 1. At this stage, you add in kissing, touching, and caressing.

- **Stage 3 – Intercourse.** The physical act of sex.

- **Stage 4 – Orgasm.** The climax of the physical act.

- **Stage 5 – Love making.** Repeat step one. This step never stops.

Most men make the mistake of thinking women experience and respond to these five stages the same way they do.

A Woman's Sexuality: What Wives Wish Their Husbands Knew

- **Stage 1** – "Lovemaking for me may take anywhere from several hours to several days. This is a never-ending process. I am unable to completely physically connect with you unless and until I am emotionally connected with you."

- **Stage 2** – "While you are easily aroused and operate like a microwave, I am slower to arouse, more like a slow cooker. This is the most important stage for me. Without proper arousal, I will not enjoy sex as much as you will, and in fact, it may actually be painful for me. So, slow your arousal down and allow me to catch up. If you get this right, everything else will fall into place."

- **Stage 3** – "Make sure we discuss which positions are comfortable or uncomfortable for me. Let's discuss sex, and not just when we are having sex."

- **Stage 4** – "It typically takes longer for me to achieve orgasm. My orgasm may be longer and more intense than yours, however. Regardless, my orgasm is important to me and I don't want you to ignore your responsibility to please me. We work together sexually as a team."

According to some studies, as many as one in three women have trouble reaching orgasm while they are having sex. As many as 80 percent of women have difficulty reaching orgasm from vaginal intercourse alone.

- **Stage 5** – "It is important for me that this never stops, all day every day."

A man can assume that sex is just as exciting for his wife as it is for him. The truth is, he is thrilled because he got to do it, and she is thrilled because she got through it. This should not be your married sex life.

A great husband – and who doesn't want to be a great husband – makes it his responsibility to make sure his wife enjoys sex as much as he does, and that her orgasm is as important as his orgasm. It is his job, his loyalty, his protection, and his patience as a man to ensure his wife reaches her full sexual potential. Also, even though a man's sexual intensity starts high, at some point a woman's sexual intensity will rise above her husband's if it is properly nurtured. We reach our sexual peaks at different times in our lives.

Advice for husbands:

While a husband needs sex to feel close to his wife, a wife needs closeness to feel like having sex with her husband. Now keep in mind "feeling like sex" or "not feeling like sex" is no excuse to withhold sex. These are just some words of wisdom to make sex exciting for the both of you.

Some everyday ways to keep your wife excited about having sex with you:

- Reassure her with words and displays of affection.

- Daily practice the "romance" of selflessness.

- Give her regular focused attention.

- Speak her love language often.

- Surprise her with gifts out of the ordinary.

- Stay actively involved in loving your children.

- Keep your relationship free of unresolved conflict.

- Establish a track record of being safe in the bedroom.

- Never force anything.

- Stay pain free.

- Know what she likes and what she doesn't like.

- Don't rush to or overly concentrate on hot spots. A licensed counselor once asked women about the "one thing" they wanted their husbands to know, and the overwhelming response was: "If I tell my husband where I really like attention (such as my breasts or clitoris), don't rush to these areas and don't completely focus on them. While these areas are exciting, they are also very sensitive and I have to be properly prepped to receive the attention."

- Use words to compliment and reassure.

- Remember to initiate conversation about sexual needs, likes, and dislikes outside the bedroom. Keep growing in your sexual insight and understanding. Seek outside help for sexual roadblocks.

The physical, emotional, psychological, and spiritual act of sex is the culmination of this entire manual.

- The relationship assessment tools allow couples to better understand each other, which leads to better sex.

- The discussion on expectations and fairytales allow couples to set the stage for transforming their minds, allowing them to have the mind of Christ and be loving and selfless during sex.

- The contract or covenant discussion reminds each spouse of his or her commitment, duties, and responsibilities during sex.

- The "communicate or your marriage will disintegrate" session teaches the importance of good communication, a valuable tool before, during, and after sex.

- The session on caring enough to embrace conflict is a preventive tool. In the midst of conflict (unresolved conflict), more than likely you will not have a great deal of sex, or you may have no sex at all.

Session 10: Sanctified, Satisfying, and Sizzling Married Sex!

- The session on being a Godly husband or Godly wife helps each spouse better understand his or her roles. If each spouse is primarily concerned with "outdoing" the other, and this attitude carries over to sex, think how amazing it will be.

- The family finances section teaches the importance of a plan, and allows each spouse to be proactive instead of reactive. This minimizes stress, and everyone knows less stress leads to better sex.

Do you see how everything we have discussed leads us to this point?

Great marriages have couples who are having great sex. Sex is a great indicator of how well things are going or not going in other areas of your marriage.

Sex is like a marriage thermometer, not a thermostat. In other words, sex (the frequency, intensity, positions, and location) is not something used to heat up a marriage. Sex is more of a gauge that accurately shows the temperature of a marriage relationship.

Remember we discussed the three purposes of marriage? Procreation, Sanctification, and Illustration

> "Sexual intimacy is more than the bringing together of sexual organs, more than the reciprocating sensual arousal of both partners, more even than mutual fulfillment in orgasm, It is the experience of sharing and self-abandon in the emerging of two persons, expressed by the biblical phrase 'to become one flesh.'"
>
> —Howard and Charlotte Clinebell

Think of sex as having three purposes, as well:

- The procreation of the species. Read Genesis 1:28 and Psalm 127:3-5. We are to produce little "image bearers" of God.

- The pleasure of the (married) people. Read Proverbs 5:18-19. God invented sex to pleasure the man and the woman.

- The protection of the institution (of marriage). Read 1 Corinthians 7:2-5. If the marriage is not sexually satisfying, one or both spouses may be tempted to look outside the marriage for sexual fulfillment.

Another question we often get is, "What is permissible in the area of Christian married sex as far as different sexual positions, sex, toys, oral sex, etc.?" Let examine.

Once, we were in the midst of pre-marital classes with two young couples, both of whom were concerned that married sex was going to be boring. They literally asked, "Do we have to have sex only in the missionary position?"

They looked at their lives as Christians the same way many others do: if something is too much fun or if we are really enjoying it, then God is probably angry. That is not how God works!

Our interaction with that young couple led us to make sure you understand your marriage "threesome" – yes, "threesome" – you, your spouse, and Christ – is not meant to be boring. It's meant to be just the opposite.

"There is nothing spiritual or moral about limiting sexual pleasure in marriage. God is the greatest proponent of your pleasure – not the pleasure that is sweet for a season, but the deep profound satisfaction that only grows sweeter with time. Clinical Psychologist Dr. Juli Slattery says, "Once we understand what God has said 'no' to, we are free to have great

Session 10: Sanctified, Satisfying, and Sizzling Married Sex!

time exploring all He has given us to enjoy."

Dr. Slattery adds:

> As with all areas of life, God's instruction on sex can be found in the Bible. The Bible talks about sex a lot, but often the answers to sexual questions aren't found in a chapter or verse – for example, you won't find any reference to vibrators. But using the Bible as a reference guide for decisions, we can make wise decisions in discerning good from evil (Hebrews 5:14), even when something seems like a gray area.

Here are three questions to help discern whether certain sexual acts are right or wrong.

Question #1 – What does God clearly say "no" to?

Fornication: which means having sex outside of marriage (I Corinthians 7:2, I Thessalonians 4:3)

Adultery: having sex with someone who is not your spouse. Jesus expanded adultery to mean not just physical acts, but emotional acts in the mind and heart (Matthew 5:28)

Homosexuality: The Bible is very clear that for a man to have sex with a man or a woman to have sex with a woman is wrong in God's eyes (Romans 1:27, I Corinthians 6:9)

Lustful Passions: First, let me tell you what this does NOT mean. Lustful passion *does not* refer to the powerful, God-given sexual desire that a married man and woman enjoy. Instead, it refers to an unrestrained, indiscriminate sexual desire for men or women other than the person's marriage partner (Mark 7:21-22, Ephesians 4:19)

Coarse Joking: In Ephesians 4:29, Paul says, "Do not let any unwholesome talk come out of your mouths." We have all been around people who can see a sexual connotation in some innocent phrase, then begin to snicker or laugh. This is wrong. This does not rule out sexual humor in the privacy of marriage, however, but rather inappropriate sexual comments in a public setting.

Question #2 – How do you keep sex just between you and your spouse?

God said "no" to having sex outside of marriage and having sex with someone you're not married to, so why do we even ask this question? Because many people fudge on it.

Reserving sex, sexual fantasies, and sexual expression only for your spouse means more than just what you do physically, but what you look at and what you think about. Jesus said in Matthew 5:27-28, "You have heard that it was said, 'Do not commit adultery.' But I tell you that anyone who looks at a woman lustfully has already committed adultery with her in his heart."

Question #3 – Will this sexual activity be good for both of us?

Not good "to," but good "for." See the difference?

That's an important distinction. This is where things get fuzzy. We don't see anywhere in the Bible where God clearly says "no" to things like sex toys, masturbation, or oral sex. In fact, you'll find very different opinions from Christian leaders on all these topics. The Corinthian church had questions about gray areas, too. Instead of telling them exactly what to do, Paul gave them guidelines on how to use good judgment when the Bible doesn't clearly state something as right or wrong.

1 Corinthians 6:12 says, "Everything is permissible for me—but not everything is beneficial. Everything is permissible for me—but I will not be mastered by anything.

Here's what you can take from this passage. There are many things in life that you are free to do and enjoy. When you are not sure whether something is okay, put it through Paul's filter:

- Is it beneficial? Is it good for me? Is it good for my spouse? Is it good for our marriage?
- Does it master me? Can it be habit-forming or addictive?
- Is it constructive? Does it help me grow and mature? Does it build our marriage?
- Is it loving? Does this action show love toward my spouse, or is it selfish?

This may mean that for some couples, a particular sexual act will be fine, but not for other couples. One example of this is oral sex. Some couples feel great freedom to include this in their lovemaking. For other couples, oral sex triggers memories of sexual abuse or pornographic images. The same act can be loving for one couple and harmful for another.

God invented sex and declared that "It is good."

Enjoy!

 To listen to the podcast with Jim and Teresa discussing this session and additional resources, go to www.RelationshipSuccessUniversity.com/bookguide.

Session 11: Prepared Parents

Our children…the messages we send to the future.

I was born in Little Rock, Arkansas, adopted when I was two weeks old, and grew up in Dorsey, Mississippi. By the grace of God, I had two great parents, not perfect parents (there are no perfect parents), but great parents.

Take your responsibility to have children seriously. Think about and prepare for parenthood.

Despite what the world tells you, Psalm 127:3 proclaims that children are a blessing from Him. If you are unable to have biological children of your own, please consider adoption. There are lots of children who would love to have you as parents. Find a reputable adoption agency in your area, like Bethany Christian Services, and start the process.

Even if you have a biological child or children, we are asking you to consider adoption. There is a huge need, especially for African American parents, to adopt.

What is the current state of our children?

Search Institute conducted a nationwide survey of 11,000 participants from 561 congregations across six different denominations. The results are alarming:

- Only 12 percent of youth have a regular dialogue with their mother on faith or life issues.
- Only 5 percent of youth have a regular dialogue with their fathers on faith or life issues.
- Only 9 percent of youth have experienced regular Bible reading and devotions in the home.
- Only 12 percent of youth have experienced a servanthood event with a parent as an action of faith.

George Barna confirmed all this in his research for his book, *Transforming Children into Spiritual Champions*:

> We discovered that in a typical week, fewer than 10 percent of parents who regularly attend church with their kids read the Bible together, pray together (other than at mealtimes) or participate in an act of service as a family unit. Even fewer families — 1 out of 20 — have any type of worship experience together with their kids, other than while they are at church during a typical month.
>
> The local church should be an intimate and valuable partner in the effort to raise the coming generation of Christ's followers and church leaders, but it is the parents whom God will hold primarily accountable for the spiritual maturation of their children.

Parents have turned over the primary responsibility of educating their children to public and private schools; the primary responsibility of entertaining their children to TV, the internet, and video games; and the primary responsibility of endearing biblical teaching and training to the local church; and the church unwittingly, unknowingly, and incorrectly accepted the job.

Faith is Caught, Not Taught!

Many teens surveyed reported that they did not stay engaged in their faith because faith was really nothing more than a program they attended. As they got older and wiser, they started to see faith as hypocritical because their parents acted one way at church and a completely different way at home.

When these teens became young adults, they concluded if this is what Christianity is about, they didn't want anything to do with it.

Session 11: Prepared Parents

How do we train our children, and what are some of the barriers?

Families are busy:

- Kids participate in a variety of extracurricular activities by the time they enter pre-school.

- Teenagers' pressured lives create stress and anxiety. Parents rush around in pursuit of the best for their children and may miss the opportunity to teach God's ways in the natural rhythms of life. There's rarely an opportunity to experience God's presence or see God at work.

Parents think discipling their children is the job of the "professionals":

- Most Christian parents' actions reveal their belief that the spiritual growth of their children is the primary responsibility of trained specialists.

- Just as parents take their children to soccer practice to be taught by a trained coach and piano lessons to be taught by a professional, they take their children to church to be discipled. This view is only half true – the church and parents work together.

Parents aren't sure how to be the primary faith influencers: Training a child spiritually seems frightening and foreign to the average parent. Many parents have no idea what it looks like to teach their children to relate to God through the life, death, and resurrection of Jesus. It's rare to find a 30- or 40-something parent who understands the practice of impressing God's commands on their children in daily life. This is a problem that we as community leaders can address.

Notes

Becoming a Prepared Parent

Read Proverbs 22:6.

Discuss the practical application of this verse in your role and responsibility as a parent.

What does "the way he should go" mean?

As you might expect the Bible has a lot to say about preparing parents to lead their children to discipleship. Several years ago I attended the D6 conference in Plano, Texas, with several thousand of my closest friends. The focus of the conference was the passage Deuteronomy 6. Visit them at www.d6family.com.

Session 11: Prepared Parents

> Hear, O Israel: The LORD our God, the LORD is one. Love the LORD your God with all your heart and with all your soul and with all your strength. These commandments that I give you today are to be on your hearts. Impress them on your children. Talk about them when you sit at home and when you walk along the road, when you lie down and when you get up. Tie them as symbols on your hands and bind them on your foreheads. Write them on the doorframes of your houses and on your gates.
>
> -- Deuteronomy 6:4-9 (NIV)

Let's visit the original blueprint and learn how to adopt and practice this instructional passage for the sake of our children and generations to come. Families were designed with relationships in mind. Children are dependent on those relationships for their physical, emotional, and spiritual development. From birth, everything we do as parents leaves an impression, so D6 is about ensuring those impressions are founded in a scriptural understanding of our responsibility to disciple our children.

God created the family so His name could be passed down through the ages, generation by generation (see the D6 passage). No one has more spiritual influence on the life of a child than his or her parents; therefore, it is of the utmost importance that parents are equipped to fulfill the commands in D6.

Whether you are a young couple just starting a family, an established family with its own set of challenges, or parents who have become grandparents, it's never too late to begin applying these principles taught in D6.

The overriding theme of this passage is to be constant and intentional. Let's look at some practical insights from God's Word as we unpack our responsibility to impress the Gospel on the next generation.

Notes

Rules without relationship lead to rebellion. The first person I ever heard say that was Josh McDowell and it makes so much sense. Children, or people in general for that matter, don't respond well to a bunch of do's and don'ts without the formation of a real relationship. Take a relational approach to parenting your children. Think of the word "Relationships" as an acronym:

Relational approach
Encouragement
Laughter and celebration
Acceptance
Transparency
Involvement of today's technology
Outreach (invite their friends over and make your home the gathering place for the group)
Nurturing
Spiritual growth
Have a happy home
Intimacy
Personal Attention
Strategic follow-up to the intentional approach

The best way to help children grow spiritually is to touch them through relationships. You don't have to always look for special activities just for them. Include them in your life, and use those opportunities to teach life lessons.

What you do is speaking so loudly that they can't hear what you are saying. In other words, be the change that you want to see. Your conduct and your conversation must match. Your children are watching you and will grow up to be very much like you "for better or worse." Your job is to minimize the damage they mimic when observing fallen sinful people and maximize the influence of the Christ!

Demonstrate the Gospel While You Declare the Gospel

While you don't have to be perfect as a parent, you do have to be real. While you can fool some of the people all of the time and all of the people some of the time, you can't kid a kid!

Be intentional. Our family loves to take road trips. One spring we took a drive to Toronto, Canada. We carefully planned our stops and sights to see along the way. We spent the night in Louisville, Kentucky, and later spent the night in Buffalo, New York, to visit Niagara Falls. And of course, even when we weren't stopping to spend the night someplace, we still took bathroom breaks and stopped for gas. We had a lot of fun on the trip, but make no mistake, the goal was to ultimately end up in Toronto, Canada. Raising our children happens much the same way as a road trip. We laugh; we play; and we have fun; but at the end of the day, our goal is to make disciples.

Being intentional focuses on using every opportunity to reinforce foundational principles to children both in formal and informal ways. Maybe it's having intentional times set aside each week for conversation based on scripture. Maybe it's a walk to the park or a trip to the mall. Look for "real life" opportunities to teach core competencies in informal ways by modeling and speaking truth. These opportunities are things that happen as we walk along the road of life, as we lie down, and as we get up.

Use every opportunity to teach or remind your children of a spiritual principle.

Notes

The best thing a man can do for his children is to let them see him love his wife. I talk with young people all the time, whether it be our own children and their friends, or through one of our public school partnerships. Over and over I hear these young people voice concerns about getting married because their parents have had bad marriages.

Our oldest daughter told me just recently she is not going to marry a man until she finds one who will treat her like she saw her dad treat her mom. This is not something I told her and coerced her into saying; it's a conclusion she has drawn after watching her parents' marriage for 29 years. Teresa is constantly singing my praises to the children because of how I treat her.

Children need to feel safe, secure, and significant. A man who loves his wife will help ensure that the children feel safe, secure, and significant:

- **Safe** – no matter what is going on at school and in the world, our home is a safe place.

- **Secure** – our home is not going anywhere. My mom is not leaving and my dad is not leaving. I feel secure here.

- **Significant** – I matter here, and I know I matter because my parents constantly tell me that I matter, that they love me, that they are proud of me, and that God has a special plan for me.

Teach your children not only how to count, but more importantly, what counts. As we write this, Jeremy is finishing up a Master's in Industrial Psychology, Madison is finishing a Master's in Accounting, Elizabeth is preparing to go to Graduate School in Switzerland, and Jimmie is constantly seeking educational materials to assist in his Real Estate Investment company. So we are obviously proponents of a person getting an education.

Session 11: Prepared Parents

But more important than their future career goals, we are concerned about our children's moral character and their Christian world life view. Have you ever noticed when you ask parents about their children, they begin to tell you about some recent accomplishment like their acceptance into some program, or their exploits on the playing field?

There's nothing wrong with that as long as we keep it in the proper perspective. I know your child is an "A" student, but what is his or her grade in holding fast to the foundations of the faith in the midst of mixed signals – signals that send a message contrary to what Christ teaches? What's your child's grade in Applied Christianity?

Teach your children not only the cost of things, but more importantly, the value of things. Teach them:

- A reverence for God (Proverbs 1:7)

- A right understanding of obedience to God's Word (Exodus 20:12, the Fifth Commandment)

- Relational purity (Proverbs 2:1-19 and Proverbs 2:20). God is not keeping sex from your children; He is keeping sex for them. Teach them what the Word of God says about sex. Rather than teach about sexually transmitted diseases and premature pregnancies (both realities of sex outside the confines of marriage) actually teach them what the word sex means. Ultimately you are not trying to influence only their behavior; you're trying to get them to base their core beliefs on the Word of God.

- Rules about money (Proverbs 3:9) – make sure they leave home with certain basic money skills; for example, make sure they know how to balance a checkbook, reconcile a bank statement, and set up a spending plan (budget).

- Requirements to work (Proverbs 6:9)

- Regrets of not choosing Godly friends (Proverbs 13:20)

Be a PAL to your child:

- **P**resent – be around your children; do activities together.
- **A**vailable – always be available to your children; it allows them to see your true priorities.
- **L**istening – I would say more, but I want you to "just do it," not read about it.

Family meals together – When our children were growing up, we tried to eat as many meals together as possible, but with four children at various ages, involved in various activities, we couldn't always eat one or two meals together every day. We did have one meal that was non-negotiable, however – Sunday meals after church. Every Sunday, as far back I as can remember, we sat down together for a family meal. This is not a time to discipline and correct; it's a time of fellowship, and as the children got older, it became a time of discussion on real and relevant issues.

To this day when I ask our children about their memories of growing up in our house, all of them mention the times we spent together at the table on Sundays being some of their fondest memories. Once the children were older and the conversation was more adult in nature, many a Sunday dinner saw us sitting around the table for two or three hours just laughing and talking.

Most Sundays after family time, others dropped by and the conversation continued. Priceless time. After all, it is in the family "where life is making up its mind."

Charles Swindoll said:

> "Whatever else may be said about the home, it is the bottom line of life, the anvil upon which attitudes and convictions are hammered out. It is the place where life's bills come due, the single most influential force in our earthly existence.......It is at home among family members, that

we come to terms with circumstances. It is here, life makes up its mind."

> "Discipline is not a necessary evil; it is a necessary good because of evil. Discipline is a virtue, a positive promoter of spirituality, morality, and relational integrity, which the Bible refers to as righteousness."
>
> – Doug Fields

Family devotions – make sure they are regular, the appropriate length, (which has a lot to do with the age of the children); and involve them (let them select songs, Bible verses, or stories they are interested in). Engage your older children in real-life decisions and struggles and find a Bible passage, story, or truth that speaks to those struggles.

Discipline your children:

There is a distinguishable difference between discipline and punishment, even though most people use the two words interchangeably.

Discipline is proactive, sets boundaries, and provides positive guidance.

Punishment is reactive, implements the consequences of going beyond boundaries, and is positive reinforcement.

Discipline is defined as "the practice of training people to obey rules or codes of behavior, using punishment to correct disobedience."

Punishment is part of discipline but not the same as discipline. When we discipline our children we are literally making little disciples. Discipline comes from the same root as *disciple*, which means "follower" or "learner."

Did your parents understand the difference between discipline and punishment?

___ Yes ___ No

How were you disciplined as a child?

_____

_____

_____

_____

How were you punished as a child?

_____

_____

_____

_____

How does that differ from how your spouse was disciplined?

_____

_____

_____

_____

Session 11: Prepared Parents

Rules for disciplining children – Proverbs 13:24 says, "Whoever spares the rod hates their children, but the one who loves their children is careful to discipline them."

- Set boundaries.
- Expect good behavior.
- Recognize good behavior.
- Have a few simple rules.
- Explain rules positively and explain their purpose.
- Make sure the consequences are appropriate and known ahead of time.
- Know the difference between annoying (what you don't like) and inappropriate (what is wrong).
- Minimize your warnings for misbehavior.
- Enforce rules without anger.
- Don't embarrass your children.
- Discipline collectively as a parental team.

We talk to parents all the time who are against most forms of punishment, especially corporal punishment (i.e. spanking, whipping, using a belt or switch, etc.) Most parents who are against corporal punishment had really bad experiences with the way their own parents applied punishment. Just because you were the "victim" of a really bad pattern of punishment, that does not make punishment (corporal or otherwise) a bad idea.

You have heard people say they don't go to church because of all the hypocrites there. Well, if that's the reason (and it's not, by the way; it's just an excuse), why not burn or throw away all of the $20 bills in your wallet since the $20 bill is the most counterfeited (hypocritical) bill in circulation in the United States?

The answer is just because one person or a group of people are wrong in the way they handle something, that doesn't make that particular thing or situation wrong.

Notes

Rules for punishing children:

Punishment should be progressive – don't jump to corporal punishment "right off the bat" and especially for minor offenses (unless they are repeat offenses).

Before moving to corporal punishment, try one of the many other techniques that might be effective, depending on the child:

- Taking away privileges
- Assigning unpleasant duties
- Restrictions

What are some methods of punishment you can administer before you administer corporal punishment?

_____

_____

_____

_____

_____

As the head of our house, whenever (well, most of the time) I was about to administer corporal punishment, I asked my child a series of questions. This served two purposes:

1. It allowed me to restate or reinforce the rule that was broken, which led to the punishment I was about to deal out.

2. It allowed both myself and the child to grade me on how well I had done my job as leader of this family.

The conversation would typically go like this:

Session 11: Prepared Parents

ME: Dorothy, did Dad explain why this behavior or action was wrong (don't blame the child if you haven't done your job in instructing him or her). *By the way we don't have child named Dorothy; the names of the children have all been changed in this reenactment to protect the guilty.*

DOROTHY: Yes, Dad, you were very clear on why this is not acceptable. (If the child says "no," assuming he or she is being truthful (children will be dishonest, but that's another subject for another chapter), then examine yourself and determine how effective and INTENTIONAL you have been in providing instruction and training.

ME: Did Dad explain what the consequences would be if you were in violation of this rule/principle/concept?

DOROTHY: Yes, Dad. (Again if the answer is "no," that's your responsibility.)

ME: So if Dad explained why this was wrong and what would happen if you chose to do the wrong thing, the fact that you are about to get a spanking is not like I'm spanking you; it's really like you are spanking yourself.

Discuss the above example.

Rules for spanking:

- Spanking is never done when you are angry.
- Spanking is only administered after the child has been previously instructed and warned.
- Spanking should include more positives than negatives. (As part of the discipline process, be verbally positive, as opposed to belittling and embarrassing the child).
- Spanking is to correct, not to retaliate.
- Spanking should not ever escalate to abuse.
- Spanking must be age appropriate.
- Every child has a designated "spanking place."
- Don't make one parent the designated spanker.

- Spanking should be done in conjunction with teaching.
- Don't be angry after you have spanked – you are teaching consequences, repentance, and forgiveness.

God doesn't stop loving us because He has to punish us. He doesn't stop loving us just because we are "bad." That is the example you want to model with your children.

Catch your children doing something right (the principle of encouragement) – Understand the power of words and use them wisely. See James 3:1-12.

Make learning fun for your children – When I was growing up, I watched *Fat Albert* on television every Saturday morning. As an overweight kid, I actually hated that show, but I do remember Bill Cosby saying each morning that we were going to have a lot of fun and if I wasn't careful, I might learn something. That's the attitude we take with instructing our children. It's fun; it's intentional; and it's instructional.

Pray – Pray for your children and with your children. Teach them how to pray. Let them see you praying. I can't tell you how many mornings our children walked out of their bedrooms to find me in my "special place," down on my knees or flat on my face, praying. I can't tell you how often their mother tells them, "I am praying for you" followed by the specifics of what she is praying.

Scripture memorization and teaching a world and life view:

Catechism – Through a series of questions, a child learns what to believe and more importantly WHY to believe it.

What is Catechism?

Catechism is simply a systematic approach using questions and answers to teach. In Zacharias Ursinus' *Heidelberg Catechism*,

Session 11: Prepared Parents

he explains:

> The system of catechizing...includes a short, simple, single, and plain exposition of rehearsal of the Christian doctrine, deduced from the writings of prophets and apostles, and arranged in the form of questions and answers, adapted to the capacity and comprehension of the ignorant and unlearned; or it is a brief summary of the doctrine of the prophets and apostles communicated orally to such as are unlearned, which they are again required to repeat.

Ultimately catechism is a means of teaching Christian doctrine in a concise, repetitive manner.

Martin Luther wrote, "In the catechism we have a very exact, direct, and short way to the whole Christian religion."

The job of parents is to teach their children how to believe like Christians and to behave like Christians.

It's one thing to tell your high school student who has to deal with public school teaching on evolution that the teacher is wrong. It's another thing to have taught your child Genesis 1:27, Colossians 3:10, and Ephesians 4:24 since he or she was old enough to walk.

Choose the appropriate age (remember children can learn more and learn faster than we often give them credit for), and teach your child(ren) to learn a set number of questions each week, month, and year.

Remember to encourage and reward them for their efforts, and make the learning fun. You could start with two or three questions until both you and you children have mastered all 105 questions and answers.

The series of questions that make up the Catechism is appropriate for two-year-olds.

Some examples of the questions and answers are:

1. Q. Who made you?

    A. God made me (Genesis 1:26, 27; 2:7; Ecclesiastes 12:1; Acts 17:24-29).

2. Q. What else did God make?

    A. God made all things (Genesis 1, esp. verses 1, 31; Acts 14:15; Romans 11:36; Colossians 1:16).

3. Q. Why did God make you and all things?

    A. For his own glory (Psalm 19:1; Jeremiah 9:23, 24; Revelation 4:11).

4. Q. How can you glorify God?

    A. By loving him and doing what he commands (Ecclesiastes 12:13; Mark 12:29-31; John 15:8-10; 1 Corinthians 10:31).

5. Q. Why should you glorify God?

    A. Because he made me and takes care of me (Romans 11:36; Revelation 4:11; cf. Daniel 4:37).

6. Q. Is there more than one god?

    A. There is only one God (Deuteronomy 6:4; Jeremiah 10:10; Mark 12:29; Acts 17:22-31).

7. Q. Into how many persons is God divided?

    A. In three persons (Matthew 3:16, 17; John 5:23; 10:30; 4:9, 10; 15:26; 16:13-15; 1 John 5:20; Revelation 1:4, 5).

8. Q. Who are they?

    A. The Father, the Son, and the Holy Spirit (Matthew 28:19; 2 Corinthians 13:14; 1 Peter 1:2; Jude 1:20, 21).

9. Q. Who is God?

    A. God is a Spirit, and does not have a body like men (John 4:24; 2 Corinthians 3:17; 1 Timothy 1:17).

10. Q. Where is God?

    A. God is everywhere (Psalms 139:7-12; Jeremiah 23:23, 24; Acts 17:27, 28).

Session 11: Prepared Parents

11. Q. Can you see God?

    A. No. I cannot see God, but he always sees me (Exodus 33:20; John 1:18; 1 Timothy 6:16; Psalm 139 esp. vv. 1-5; Proverbs 5:21; Hebrews 4:12, 13).

12. Q. Does God know all things?

    A. Yes. Nothing can be hidden from God (1 Chronicles 28:9; 2 Chronicles 16:9; Luke 12:6, 7; Romans 2:16).

13. Q. Can God do all things?

    A. Yes. God can do all his holy will (Psalm 147:5; Jeremiah 32:17; Daniel 4:34, 35; Ephesians 1:11).

As Dr. Voddie Baucham writes in his book, *Family Shepherds: Calling and Equipping Men to Lead Their Homes*:

> This isn't rocket science; these are rudimentary statements. However, they get to the heart of what we believe about the nature of God (the trinity), the nature of man (a created being), and the purpose of creation (the glory of God).
>
> There are over one hundred questions in this catechism covering the basics of systematic theology. As a result, the catechumen (or pupil) – who will probably take a number of years to remember the entire catechism – will have a firm theological foundation to work from by the time he or she is done. Moreover, the catechist (or instructor) – who will have taught these things hundreds of times by asking the questions, hearing the responses, and correcting wrong answers – will most assuredly have catechized himself in the process.

This presents the perfect opportunity for both the parent and child to grow and learn. When we talk about family faith, everyone wins.

 To listen to the podcast with Jim and Teresa discussing this session and additional resources, go to www.RelationshipSuccessUniversity.com/bookguide.

Session 12: The Blended/Bonded Family: "We Do...Again"

Jim and I did a podcast where we interviewed Janice Love and we discussed the issue of step-parenting, step-families, and remarriage. The show was such a huge hit we asked the Love's to co-author this chapter on The Blended/Bonded Family. By co-author we mean they wrote practically the entire chapter. While we have counseled numerous couples about to remarry and/or dealing with related parenting issues, we haven't actually lived it.

We thought it would add tremendous value to hear from trained experts in this space and a couple who has personally traveled this road. The Love's are experienced and certified qualifying them as an amazing resource.

Step with Love Ministries – Rev. Dr. Bobby L. Love and Janice R. Love – Cofounders

Rev. Dr. Bobby L. Love Sr. is the Senior Pastor of the Historic Second Baptist Church of Olathe, Kansas, serving for the past twenty-five years. He is a (N.C.C.A.) Licensed Clinical Pastoral Counselor with Advanced Certification, with a Professional Clinical membership and is a member of the Sarasota Academy of Christian Counseling (S.A.C.C.)

Janice R. Love is the best-selling author of One Plus One Equals Ten: A First Lady's Survival Guide for Stepmoms. Her second book which ministers to divorced women is entitled: Divorced and Still Highly Favored was just released. Janice is currently pursuing a doctorate in Christian Counseling.

After experiencing the unique challenges of a blended family of eight children, Bobby and Janice trained at the world renowned Stepfamily foundation, Inc. and successfully earned credentials as a Certified Stepfamily Counselor and Coach respectively. They established Step with Love: a ministry that offers family counseling, coaching and seminars for individuals, couples and marriage ministries. This dynamic couple also provides assistance to churches, particularly Pastors and wives offering enlightenment on the unique dynamics of being in the ministry. Step with Love (SWL) recently established The Midwest Christian Counseling and Training Center, which serves as the training arm of SWL offering quality Christian Counseling training and degree programs for those who desire to become better equipped to serve their congregations and communities. The Love's reside in Olathe, Kansas.

In every conceivable manner, the family is the link to our past, bridge to our future. ~Alex Haley

Remarriage is a marriage that takes place after another marriage has ended. While some people remarry due to widowhood, the majority of remarriages happen because of divorce. Either way, if you find yourself at the door of remarriage, know that you must enter the new union prayerfully and with eyes wide open.

Widows/Widowers

In many cases widowed are older in age. However, with so many chronic diseases including cancer, widowed individuals are getting younger and younger. The most important issue if you are widowed is to take the time you need to grieve the loss of your loved one. There are no rules and timelines that you must follow and everyone grieves differently.

If you were married "until death do us part" you are a marriage expert and know what it takes to have a long lasting marriage. However, loneliness and difficulty transitioning to single life leads some to marry too soon or select the wrong person. Widowed men will remarry more often than women, but overall the average adult who remarries has known his or her new spouse less than nine months. When beginning a new relationship, take your time and don't rush into anything.

Once remarried be careful to not continuously live in the past. Pay special attention to your surroundings so that your new spouse feels welcomed. Help your children to make the adjustment by sharing the value your new spouse adds to your life, but don't force relationships. Most of all avoid comparisons and expectations based on your first marriage or spouse.

Remarriage Following Divorce

As already mentioned the majority of remarriages occur because of divorce. Even though divorce rates are lower, it is still predicted that 35% – 45% of marriages will end in divorce. Statistics for second and third marriages are grim especially when children are involved with failure rates as high as 66%. Some couples are afraid of remarrying and will cohabitate with their new partner and their children. Couples with children who remarry may refer to themselves as a "blended family", "stepfamily" or the latest term "bonus family". For the purposes of this document we will use the term stepfamilies. Here are some statistics related to remarriages with children.

- About 60 percent of all second remarriages end in divorce, and about 75 percent of all third marriages end in divorce.
- About 75 percent of divorced people eventually remarry.
- About 43 percent of all marriages are remarriages for at least one of the spouses involved.
- About 65 percent of remarriages involve children from a prior marriage and form blended families.
- 1300+ new re-coupled families form every day.

Notes

Considering Remarriage?

If you are preparing to marry again or marry someone who has already been married, you are not alone. Stepfamilies are challenging particularly if you try to manage this unique family the same way you managed your original family. The last place you want to be is back in divorce court, so it is important to not rush into marriage. If you are recently divorced, don't rush into another relationship. Take the time to evaluate your life and your choices and what went wrong in your last marriage. For your children's sake don't consider marriage until at least two years have passed. Divorce is a difficult adjustment for children and they need time to adjust before you introduce a new parental figure in their life.

Take some time to do some self-reflection and answer the following questions.

What are your beliefs about love and marriage? What did you learn about love and marriage in your family of origin that I carried over into your previous marriage?

_____

_____

_____

What went wrong in your previous marriage? What will you do differently if you marry again?

_____

_____

_____

Where are you in your faith journey? Do you trust that God will provide for you regardless of your circumstances? Do you believe that God still loves you even though you are divorced? Do you believe that God is mad at you? Do you trust that God has your best interest at heart?

_____

_____

_____

Review the following scriptures: 2 Corinthians 13:5-7, Job 13:23, Psalm 26:2, Psalm 4:4, Lamentations 3:40 (CEB), Psalm 119:59 (TLB)

Session 12: The Blended/Bonded Family: "We Do...Again!"

The Second Wedding

Decided you are ready to be re-married? Start off the right way this time. Consider these 7 tidbits of advice in preparation for your remarriage.

1. Premarital Counseling

Seek structured pre-marital counseling from your pastor or a Christian counselor as soon as you are engaged. Find a pastor and counselor trained in stepfamily dynamics.

- Begin counseling 8 to 10 months before the wedding date.
- Read a stepfamily book (One Plus One +Equals Ten: A First Lady's Survival Guide for Stepmoms) by Janice R. Love

Who will do your Counseling? Do they have the knowledge and tools to help stepfamilies?

_____

_____

2. Communicate with Bio-Parents

Talk with your children's biological parents about getting married and the children's involvement in the ceremony.

- Discuss how to inform the children about the upcoming marriage.
- If the non-marrying spouse discusses the pending marriage with children they will have the opportunity to vent their true feelings without feeling like they are offending the parent.
- Avoid possible sabotage by having conversations in advance.

Meeting time and place?

_____

_____

3. Talk with Your Children & Listen

Discuss your marriage plans with your children even if you plan to elope. Never marry without informing them of your plans.

- Inform them of the facts including date, time and location.
- Talk with each child individually to sort out their feelings about the upcoming marriage. Ask how they feel. Be careful that it does not appear that you are asking for their permission.
- Remember kids prefer to have their biological parents back together.
- Allow them to decide if they want to participate in the wedding. If they chose not to participate, it is okay. Remind them still love them.

How did children respond to your announcement? How will children participate in the wedding?

_____

_____

4. Keep it Simple

Keep the wedding plans as simple as possible.

- Decide if you will have a large wedding or a small intimate one.
- Research second wedding ceremonies including vows.
- Consider vows or dedications to the children if appropriate.

What did you learn from researching second weddings?

_____

_____

5. Be Flexible

- Be prepared for last minute changes or sabotage.
- Beware of ex-spouse sabotage such as not allowing child to attend wedding. The child may feel guilty change his or her mind and decide not to attend or participate.
- Avoid crossfire by paying for everything so the ex does not incur any costs associated with your wedding.

6. Plan a Honeymoon

- Get away for at least 5 days to a week to build couple strength.
- Going away alone emphasizes to everyone the importance of your alone time and validation of your new life together.
- Make arrangements with ex-spouse or grandparents to care for children while you are away.

What are your honeymoon plans?

_____

_____

7. Enjoy Your Wedding Day

- Enjoy your day and don't let anyone or anything spoil it!
- Remember not everyone may be as excited as you are about the wedding.
- Concentrate on enjoying your wedding and making happy memories.
- Smile and keep smiling, even when children or others may not smile with you.

How to Have a Successful Remarriage and Stepfamily

Remarriage and bringing two families together can be highly rewarding and a blessing for all involved. However, being a stepfamily can be tough. Let me encourage you by stating what many pastors and religious leaders will not tell you. Many churches unknowingly ignore stepfamilies and on occasion, treat them as second class church members. When you look at the overall make up of today's church, you may be surprised to learn that many of your leaders are in fact the products of stepfamily situations. You see, the sad fact is, many people do not and will not identify themselves as a stepfamily because are afraid of the ill treatment that is associated with the term stepfamily. But, have no fear about being a stepfamily because as mentioned previously, there are more than 1300 created each day. Remember, you are not alone.

With that being said, here is a brief illustration to assist you in gaining the proper perspective of what it is like living "in-step". Just think for a moment, imagine you are a kidney transplant candidate who was just notified that a donor match has been found. Following the surgery, everything is functioning well and you are relieved to know that the transplant was successful. Your doctor begins to explain that although your new kidney is doing what it is supposed to do, there are some complications. Your body is used the old kidney even though it wasn't functioning properly and does not want to accept the new kidney. Even though the new kidney is working, because it is foreign, your immune system suspects an intruder and tries to destroy it. Your physician informs you that he or she has to prescribe anti-rejection medicine so that your body will tolerate your new kidney and function as it is supposed to. The medication will actually suppresses the immune system and to allow it to accept the new kidney. You now understand that for the rest of your life you will be subject to anti-rejection medication in order for your body to function properly.

This is exactly what happens when a new stepfamily comes into being. A couple finds that they are perfect for one another (match) and decided to take their relationship to the next level and get married (transplant). Once married, the new family unit (kidney) begins to try to function in its new environment (host recipient). Before long, the family experiences challenges (rejection) especially as it relates to the children. An intervention (antibiotic) is strongly needed and the couple must seek the assistance of stepfamily specialists (physicians) to assist them with a family survival plan (prescription). Without understanding the dynamics of living in-step and getting the proper help, the couple may continue to struggle and end up divorced (kidney failure).

Hopefully this illustration has given you a look into the challenges couples face when individuals with children from a previous relationship come together and marry. We don't have enough space to cover everything, but here are ten survival tips for remarried couples living in-step.

To listen to the podcast with Jim and Teresa discussing this session and additional resources, go to www.RelationshipSuccessUniversity.com/bookguide.

Session 13: Making Godly Decisions: Are You Sure You Want To Do This?

This question is not meant to frighten you. It's simply to make you think. What you are about to do is serious. It's a covenant, not a contract, and it is not breakable. This is for the rest of your life, 'til death do you part, for better or worse, in sickness and in health.

We have counseled many a couple, who, after completing this course, realized that marriage may not be a good idea at this time or to this person. In other words, the course did its job in forcing the participants to look closely and carefully at themselves, and many times what they saw was not encouraging.

But we have couples who had second thoughts and were still determined to get married. The "crazy" reasons they gave included:

"Whatever you say do Lord, I will do"

- We have already ordered wedding invitations.
- We have already booked and paid for the reception hall.
- It will be embarrassing to call off the wedding at this late date.
- I really want to be married.
- My mom will be disappointed.

If you are having second thoughts about getting married, read and follow the instructions in this session.

Marriage done right is a wonderful thing. Marriage done wrong is miserable!

At this point in the study, what have you learned about yourself and each other that concerns you?

_____
_____
_____

What are some areas that may require special attention?

_____
_____
_____

What are some areas you need to grow in?

_____
_____
_____

What have you learned about your prospective spouse during this study that you didn't previously know?

_____
_____
_____

Are there areas that are going to require special attention?

_____
_____
_____

Session 13: Making Godly Decisions: Are You Sure You Want To Do This? 187

What are those areas?

_____

_____

_____

Here are a couple of profound questions:

Based on what you have observed and what you know about this person, are you prepared and committed to marry and live the rest of your life with this person, even if he or she does not change at all?

_____

_____

_____

Based on the baggage you see (and we all have baggage) would you marry this person right now based on what you know and see?

_____ Yes _____ No

At some point everyone considering marriage has probably asked the question "Is this relationship going to lead to marriage"? For the Christian, the question should be, "Is this the person God wants me to marry"?

How can you know that answer? How can you hear the voice and will of God in this very important decision? This session is to help you bring clarity as you seek to discern God's will for this relationship.

The purpose of this entire resource has been to allow you to see and hear clearly.

Basically this session boils down to the fundamental issue- What is God saying about this relationship?

I pray you did not come simply to fulfill a requirement with an already made up mind, but rather that you came to hear very clearly from the Lord on this matter of your relationship.

God does in fact answer every prayer of the believer. His answers are "Yes," "No," or "Wait." As a matter of fact, Bill Hybels, the founding and senior pastor of Willow Creek Community Church in South Barrington, Illinois, one of the most attended churches in North America, with an average attendance of over 25,000, says it best. I love this quote:

If the request is wrong, God says NO, If the timing is wrong, God says SLOW,

If you are wrong, God says GROW.

But if the request is right, the timing is right and you are right, God says, GO.

God does speak to people and He wants to speak to you, especially when it comes to your relationships, starting with your personal relationship (vertical) with His Son –Jesus and extending to your relationships with friends, family, and especially who you are considering marrying and/or are already married to (horizontal). God wants to speak with you, commune with you. How can we be certain?

Well let's examine the evidence. The evidence is clear:

God loves you – John 3:16 – For God so loved the world (that's you and me) that he gave his one and only Son, that whoever (that's you and me again) believes in him shall not perish but have eternal life.

We can trust God – Psalms 33:4-6 – 4 For the word of the LORD is right and true; he is faithful in all he does. 5 The LORD loves righteousness and justice; the earth is full of his unfailing love. 6 By the word of the LORD were the heavens made, their starry host by the breath of his mouth.

God cannot lie – Hebrews 6:18 God did this so that, by two unchangeable things in which it is impossible for God to lie, we who have fled to take hold of the hope set before us may be greatly encouraged.

Numbers 23:19 God is not human, that he should lie, not a human being, that he should change his mind. Does he speak and then not act? Does he promise and not fulfill?

God knows more than we do – Hebrews 4:13 – Nothing in all creation is hidden from God's sight. Everything is uncovered and laid bare before the eyes of him to whom we must give account.

God wants the best for us – John 10:10 The thief cometh not, but for to steal, and to kill, and to destroy: I am come that they might have life, and that they might have it more abundantly

Notes

Notes

Jeremiah 29:11

For I know the plans I have for you," says the Lord. "They are plans for good and not for disaster, to give you a future and a hope.

Matthew 11:28-29

Come to me, all you who are weary and burdened, and I will give you rest. Take my yoke upon you and learn from me, for I am gentle and humble in heart, and you will find rest for your souls.

Philippians 4:19

And this same God who takes care of me will supply all your needs from his glorious riches, which have been given to us in Christ Jesus.

Since God loves us, He speaks to us. Since we can trust God and He is unable to lie, we know what He is saying is true. Since God knows everything and wants the best for us, we can also be sure what He is saying to us is for our good.

There are at least three reasons it's important to hear God's voice

1. It confirms you are in God's family.

Suppose you say you are great friends with Will and Jada Pinkett Smith. As a matter of fact, you consider Denzel Washington and his wife Pauletta to be among your best of friends. You email them all the time. But the thing is, they never write you back. If you contact a person all the time and you never hear back from them, you don't have relationship.

Your aren't friends with them. You are just fans of theirs.
John 10:27 My sheep listen to my voice; I know them, and they follow me.

God doesn't only speak to certain people. If I call one of our children on the phone, they will immediately recognize my voice. As a baby this wasn't always the case. Infants don't always recognize their father's voice, but as they grow, they begin to recognize your voice. So as we grow spiritually we are better able to recognize the voice of God.

2. It protects me from mistakes.

If you will listen, Proverbs 3:6 tells us that God will warn you before you make mistakes. Sometimes this warning comes in the form of just a single word – "Don't."

Notes

3. It produces personal success.

Psalms 32:8 – I will instruct you and teach you in the way you should go; I will counsel you with my loving eye on you

Not the world's definition of success but God's definition. He has a plan for you. God's plan for me is better than my plan for me. We have all the equipment we need to hear God, we just need to learn how to tune into it.

Do you remember the story in 1 Kings 19: 10-13? The LORD Appears to Elijah:

And the word of the LORD came to him: "What are you doing here, Elijah?"

10 He replied, "I have been very zealous for the LORD God Almighty. The Israelites have rejected your covenant, torn down your altars, and put your prophets to death with the sword. I am the only one left, and now they are trying to kill me too."

11 The LORD said, "Go out and stand on the mountain in the presence of the LORD, for the LORD is about to pass by."

Then a great and powerful wind tore the mountains apart and shattered the rocks before the LORD, but the LORD was not in the wind. After the wind there was an earthquake, but the LORD was not in the earthquake. 12 After the earthquake came a fire, but the LORD was not in the fire. And after the fire came a gentle whisper. 13 When Elijah heard it, he pulled his cloak over his face and went out and stood at the mouth of the cave.

What can we learn from this passage of scripture? We have to be really quiet and really tuned in to hear the voice of God. Impediments to hearing the voice of God:

Distractions – Satan is an excellent diversionary tactician and often he doesn't use "bad" stuff to distract us. We can be distracted by "good" stuff. Satan knows our weaknesses and sometimes he works to trip us up with busy work (could even be church work). Many of us are so busy doing work, we don't allow anytime for God to work on us!

Competition – We have a lot of activities competing for our time and there are even competing messages about how and what to do. You remember the old bumper sticker? "God is my co-pilot!" Well God is not interested in being your co-pilot. Let Him do the driving. Decide right now to make God ruler of your life –In first place –and that decision will help defeat the competitors vying for your ear.

A lack of trust – In your heart of hearts, do you really trust God? Are you prepared to say to God, "Whatever you say do I will do" before He even speaks? Or, are your plans, your desires, so strong that they drown out the voice of God? One of the things I pray daily is- "Lord God please save me from me." I pray that because I don't completely trust me. Often I can't see clearly because my past, my wants and my desires get in my eyes and severely cloud my vision.

Notes

There are three things we can do to hear God speak:

1. Decide in advance that you're going to do whatever God tells you to do before He tells you to do it.

Many of us take the approach of asking God to speak to us and then we will compare the plans of God with the plans we have, and determine which way we will go. If you really want to hear from God, before you hear anything, make this promise to God- "Whatever you say do I will do."

2. Have a Daily Quiet Time.

Develop a daily habit of spending time alone with God. Your devotion time could include scripture reading, prayer, worship and praise music; it should include acknowledging any unconfessed sins, so your prayers are not hindered. But, make sure at some point there is a time of silence where you are listening for the still quiet voice of the Lord to speak to your heart.

3. Seek Godly Counsel.

Do you have people that you can trust to tell you the truth? Do you have people you consider to be maturing Christians? People of wisdom? Objective individuals with no personal motive or agenda other than to help you discern the will of God for your life? Go to these people spend time with them. A mature mentor (of the same sex) can be a great resource for you to help you hear God speak.

Session 13: Making Godly Decisions: Are You Sure You Want To Do This?

Step 1- The "7 Way" test below was taken from the *Daily Hope With Rick Warren Podcast* Episode titled, "Can You Hear Me Now? God Wants To Talk To You."

7 WAYS TO TEST IF YOU ARE ACCURATELY HEARING FROM GOD

To be absolutely certain that what you are hearing is from God, "YES" should be the answer to all seven questions:

1. Does it agree with the Bible?

- God's will never contradicts God's Word.
- Heaven and earth will disappear, but My words will never disappear. (Luke 21:33)

2. Will it make me more like Christ?

- Jesus should always be our standard.
- God is more interested in our character than in our comfort.
- Real wisdom from God is pure, peace-loving, submissive (humble & teachable), considerate, full of grace and mercy, impartial and sincere.

3. Do fellow mature believers confirm it?

- You can be ruined by the talk of godless people, but the wisdom of the righteous can save you. Without wise leadership, a nation falls; there is safety in having many advisers. (Proverbs 11:9 & 14)

Notes

4. Is it consistent with how God has shaped me?

- SHAPE = Spiritual gift + Heart + Ability + Personality + Experiences
- We are God's masterpiece. He has created us anew in Christ Jesus, so we can do the good things He planned for us long ago. (Ephesians 2:10)
- WORLD'S LIE: You can be anything you want to be. GOD'S TRUTH: You can be all that God shaped you to be.

5. Does it concern my responsibility?

- Listen for yourself; not for anybody else.
- When God wants to speak to you, He's going to speak to you in your current situation about the things you need to change.
- Who are you to condemn someone else's servants? Their own master will judge whether they stand or fall. And with the Lord's help, they will stand and receive His approval. (Romans 14:4)

6. Is it convicting rather than condemning?

- Conviction is used by God so that you will correct the wrong and change for the better.
- Condemnation is used by Satan so you will constantly question your worth, and also so that you will remain in bondage to your guilt from old sins.
- Always remember that God never attacks your value/worth.

7. Do I sense God's peace about it?

- For God is not a God of disorder but of peace. (1 Corinthians 14:33)
- The only time pressure that is legitimate is when we keep saying no to God, but once we say yes, the negative feeling is instantly replaced by peace.
- Don't worry about anything; instead, pray about everything. Tell God what you need, and thank Him for all he has done. Then you will experience God's peace, which exceeds anything we can understand. His peace will guard your hearts and minds as you live in Christ Jesus. (Philippians 4:6-7)

Okay we are almost done. Just a few final words. In this country many of us do this whole marriage thing backwards. For example while we are dating, nothing bothers us about our prospective mate. We laugh at stuff that's not funny. We ignore things that really bother us. In short, we pretend. But once we are married, we are easily irritated at the things that we ignored during the dating process.

Let's put first things first. Before you are married, make an honest evaluation of this relationship. Think carefully. Don't be so caught up in the "ideal" that you get married that it becomes an "ordeal" and shortly after you are looking for a "new deal." That's not God's plan. Remember a great marriage is not about turning your spouse into the person you think he/she should be. It's about listening to the voice of God and making a commitment to work on becoming the person God wants you to be.

Notes

Do you remember the story in Numbers 22 of the talking donkey? We put it below as a refresher.

Balaam's Donkey

21 Balaam got up in the morning, saddled his donkey and went with the Moabite officials. 22 But God was very angry when he went, and the angel of the LORD stood in the road to oppose him. Balaam was riding on his donkey, and his two servants were with him. 23 When the donkey saw the angel of the LORD standing in the road with a drawn sword in his hand, it turned off the road into a field. Balaam beat it to get it back on the road.

24 Then the angel of the LORD stood in a narrow path through the vineyards, with walls on both sides. 25 When the donkey saw the angel of the LORD, it pressed close to the wall, crushing Balaam's foot against it. So he beat the donkey again.

26 Then the angel of the LORD moved on ahead and stood in a narrow place where there was no room to turn, either to the right or to the left. 27 When the donkey saw the angel of the LORD, it lay down under Balaam, and he was angry and beat it with his staff. 28 Then the LORD opened the donkey's mouth, and it said to Balaam, "What have I done to you to make you beat me these three times?"

29 Balaam answered the donkey, "You have made a fool of me! If only I had a sword in my hand, I would kill you right now."

30 The donkey said to Balaam, "Am I not your own donkey, which you have always ridden, to this day? Have I been in the habit of doing this to you?"

"No," he said.

31 Then the LORD opened Balaam's eyes, and he saw the angel of the LORD standing in the road with his sword drawn. So he bowed low and fell facedown.

32 The angel of the LORD asked him, "Why have you beaten your donkey these three times? I have come here to oppose you because your path is a reckless one before me.[a] 33 The donkey saw me and turned away from me these three times. If it had not turned away, I would certainly have killed you by now, but I would have spared it."

Sometimes we think the miracles of the Bible are only things of the past. We are here to tell you this particular miracle is repeated day in and day out. If there is anything we have said in this study that you have found valuable, please note it was not us, it was God speaking through us.

If you were helped by this resource we beg you to share it with others. Encourage others to add this resource to their library and we pray that it will forever remain a part of your library and you will refer back to it often.

In the words of the multiple Grammy-Nominated Gospel singing group, The Williams Brothers, "We are just a nobody, trying to tell everybody, about somebody who will save anybody."

 To register for your free assessment additional resources, go to: www.RelationshipSuccessUniversity.com/bookguide.

WWW.FAMILYMATTERSFIRST.ORG

BUILDING RIGHTEOUS RELATIONSHIPS, MIGHTY MARRIAGES, FANTASTIC FAMILIES, AND PREPARED PARENTS

A study of Biblical history reveals the formation of three God-ordained institutions:

1. The Family
2. The Church
3. The Government

So goes the family, so goes the church, so goes government, so goes a nation. By starting with the foundation for success, FAMILY, and creating strong marriages and families, we will see the whole world changed.

At FMF, Inc., we work as agents of change by partnering at the local, regional, and national level to build strong families, ultimately laying a solid and firm foundation to impact positive radical cultural change. The Bible begins in Genesis with the marriage of a man and a woman and ends in the book of Revelation with the marriage of Christ and His bride, the Church.

We believe the family and the church are interdependent. A primary responsibility of the church is to help build Godly families, and Godly families and individual are the church.

Therefore, we are committed to providing the tools and the training to families to support the local church and the tools and training to the local church to support families.

Listen to our daily podcast on itunes or by downloading from our website. Also please share with us on Facebook and follow us on Twitter.

We love hearing from you. Please share if this study has helped, please send us your comments, questions, ideas, and suggestions. Also we would love to come into your local community to share with you. Details on inviting us are on the website.

The best time to go through this training is while you are dating and considering marriage – in other words, RIGHT NOW! As an ancient proverb reads, "For the man traveling down the wrong road, it's never too late to turn around."

Whether you're in a relationship now or want to be in one, you have come to the right place. We can help. Whether you're dating, engaged, married (happily or unhappily), or remarried, if you follow this resource, it is guaranteed to help you make the right decision about marriage, prepare you for marriage, or strengthen the marriage you are already in.

Teresa and I have been working on this manual all our married lives, not because we are really slow writers, but because this manual is the compilation of everything we have learned in our personal lives as a married couple for 30 years with four children – boy do we have some stories to tell – as well as our professional training. This book is a compilation of what we have seen work and not work in more than 20 years of practical application working with dating, engaged, married, and remarried couples.

We developed this system out of necessity. We used another manual for more than a decade until it was literally no longer available. We looked for other resources, but never found one that fit our style and that really resonated with the couples we were coaching and counseling. Finally we decided to develop our own.

We completed the first draft of this manual in 2010 and started using it in our weekend intensive sessions where Teresa and I meet with a couple for approximately 10 to 12 hours from Friday afternoon through Saturday (all day).

As we used this tool, we have been constantly writing, rewriting, and adding as questions and issues arose that we did not initially include in this resource. We would often leave the counseling room that Friday, come home, and add or modify a section based on a situation we saw or anticipated seeing the next day in the intensive. Though we have never made this tool available to anyone other than the couples we have personally worked with, our clients have urged us to share this resource, as they were genuinely moved and changed by the information contained herein.

What you hold in your hands is the result of this process.

This product was not developed in a classroom, using a lot of relationship theory, but rather forged in the crucible of real-life situations and circumstances. This resource is just the beginning of your journey through Relationship Success University.

Acknowledgments

Charles, a really good friend of mine, once told me, "You know, if you see a turtle sitting on a fence post, he didn't get there by himself; he had some help." Forgetting for a second that this story makes no sense to me – after all a turtle sitting on a fencepost? Isn't the turtle stranded? Who's going to bring him food? Why would the turtle want to be sitting on the fencepost? But I digress. I think Charles's point is that no man (or turtle) succeeds by himself. Teresa and I are standing on the shoulders of countless individuals and we want to pause and say thank you.

Dr. Jerry Young, our pastor at New Hope Church: your teachings are plain, personable, and portable. We have experienced tremendous growth under your leadership and we are forever in your debt. Special thanks to *Jacqueline Mack, MACE, Director of Christian Education at New Hope Church, Dr. Desmond Spann and his wife, Jennifer Spann, Elizabeth Adams,* the Reformed Theological Seminary faculty, staff, and especially Marriage and Family Therapy Professors and Supervisor, Dr. William Richardson, Dr. James Hurley, and Barbara Martin.

Explorers Bible Study and Kay Arthur Ministries: you were a tremendous help to a stay-at-home mom. Stephen Farrar, your book *Point Man* changed my life some 20 years ago. Robert Lewis, your book, Raising *A Modern Day Knight*, made me call and apologize to my sons for the poor job I did, even though I thought I was a pretty good dad.

Dr. Tony Evans, Dennis Rainey and *Family Life Ministries,* Focus on the Family, Dr. Voddie Bauchman, Beth Moore, and James Dobson: your radio ministries helped make our travel and family vacations time well spent.

Gary Chapman, Gary Smalley, Michael and Amy Smalley: after 30 years of studying and listening, sometimes your words became my words.

Iron Men: I learn so much from each of you every Saturday morning. My two accountability partners, Dr. Royal Walker and Charles Jackson: thank you for helping me see me.

And in memory of the best friend Teresa and I have ever had, Rhoda Dubose: we still hear your infectious laugh and encouraging spirit. We miss you and will see you soon.

To our four children, Madison, Jimmie, Jeremy, and Elizabeth: thank you for making us proud parents as we see each of you allowing the Lord to use you and your willingness to serve Him. You are the messengers we are sending to the future!

My apologies to anyone we are leaving out. It is not my intention to omit crediting anyone who has worked and is working to influence this mission.

About the Authors

Jim and Teresa Adams have been married since May 6, 1985. They have 4 children. Jim was born in Little Rock, Arkansas, and Teresa was born in Tupelo, Mississippi. Jim graduated Delta State University with a Bachelor of Arts in Marketing and is a Certified Marriage Intensive Coach. Teresa graduated from Mississippi University for Women with a Bachelor of Science in Food and Nutrition and Reformed Theological Seminary with a Master of Arts Degree in Marriage and Family Therapy. Teresa is a Licensed Professional Counselor (LPC) and a National Certified Counselor (NCC).

The Adams' are passionate about marriage and the family. They are sought-after teachers, trainers, speakers, and group facilitators and the co-founders of Family Matters First, Inc., a real and virtual counseling center dedicated to forming strategic partnerships with families and building righteous relationships, mighty marriages, fantastic families, and prepared parents.

In addition, they are the co-founders of the Relationship Success University. This online community at www.RelationshipSuccessUniversity.com offers a community of people dedicated to your marriage success. Tons of tools, including a growing video library of more than 5,000 videos featuring expert trainers, such as Nancy Leigh DeMoss, Beth Moore, Tony Evans, Gary Chapman, Gary Smalley, Chip Ingram, Frankie Chann, David Platt, and so many more.

RSU is literally an online Netflix-like community of videos, all dealing with individual growth, relationship growth, your Christian walk, parenting, marriage, dating, plus hundreds of videos to entertain and educate your children. It is all biblically based content and includes a closed Facebook community where you can ask questions of marriage professionals and marriage mentors, regular webinars based on issues you want to see addressed, live question-and-answer webinars moderated by Jim and Teresa, as well as online assessments to evaluate yourself as a wife, mother, or husband.

There's also Family Matters in the Workplace at www.FamilyMattersInTheWorkplace.org because unlike Vegas, what you do at home doesn't stay at home. It follows you to work and affects your productivity. Family Matters In The Workplace is a service targeted toward employers who really understand that strong marriages and families make corporate sense.

Church/Civic Groups

Nothing can shake up your church's mission, outreach and future growth more than divorce. If half the married couples in your congregation divorced, how would it affect the church?

Tithing, volunteerism, lay leadership, church attendance would all drop … significantly! Demand for financial assistance, childcare, and more of your time through pastoral counseling would all increase…significantly.

Make your church and your community less vulnerable by proactively focusing on improving the health and quality of your congregation's current and future marriages. Have a strong Marriage & Family Ministry!

Church-goers expect strong Marriage & Family leadership. Those who've attended Marriage Education classes confirm that it works. And half of those who've never attended Marriage Education would if it were made available to them.

As a pastor, you're busy and probably have too much to do already. And while there are other church priorities that you are working on right now, your church cannot afford to delay starting a Marriage Ministry or propelling an already existing Marriage Ministry to greater heights.

Using the *Preparing for Marriage Workbook* as the basis for a weekend of interactive training, Jim and Teresa spend Friday evenings from 6:00 to 9:00 and Saturday from 8:30 a.m. to 6:00 p.m. teaching through all the sessions that make up the manual.

The Church Marriage & Family Reformation Weekend is a systematic approach to Divorce Proof Marriages, Strengthen Families, Church, and Community by:

1. Adoption of Church Marriage Covenant
2. Hosting Weekend Reformation
3. Establishment/Enhancement of Marriage and Family Ministry
4. Implement pre-marital coaching and teaching programs
5. Provide access (virtual and real) to Marriage Mentors

We work with you to establish a conference leadership team of couples to promote the event church wide as well as city wide.

For more information please visit PreparingForMarriageBook.com

NOTES

Introduction

1. Sollee, Diane. *How to Become a Marriage Educator* (for Marriage Counselors, Clergy &/or the Public). The Coalition for Marriage, Family and Couples Education, LLC., 2015. Web. <http://www.smartmarriages.com/training.html>.

Session 2: So You Want to Get Married?

1. McBurney, M.D., Louis. "Marriage Preparation 101." *Focus on the Family*. Focus on the Family, 1992. Web. <http://www.focusonthefamily.com/marriage/preparing-for-marriage/approaching-the-wedding-day/marriage-preparation-101>.

Session 3: Great Expectations

1. Bledsoe, Jackie. "Blog – JackieBledsoe.com." *JackieBledsoecom*. JackieBledsoe.com. Web. <http://jackiebledsoe.com/blog/>.

2. Baker, Bob. "Fresh Start Marriage." *Fresh Start Marriage*. Marriage Foundations of Colorado Erie, 2012. Web. <http://freshstartmarriage.com/blog/>.

3. Popenoe, David, and Barbara Dafoe Whitehead. "Smart Marriages®." *Smart Marriages*. The Coalition of Marriage, Family and Couples Education, LLC., 1999. Web. <http://smartmarriage.com/cohabit.html>.

Session 4: Lose Your Mind if You Want to Love Your Spouse

1. Warren, Rick. "Biblical Marriage – On Mission Together." *Biblical Marriage – On Mission Together*. Daily Hope Ministries, 21 May 2014. Web. <http://rickwarren.org/devotional/english/biblical-marriage---on-mission-together>.

2. Lovern, Angel. "I Heard a Knock." 16 May 2005.

Session 5: Do You Know What You Are About to Do? Covenant or Contract?

1. Rainey, Dennis. "The Covenant of Marriage: Truth That Can Transform Your Marriage." *The Covenant of Marriage.* 21 Feb. 2015. Web. <http://www.preceptaustin.org/the_covenant_of_marriage.htm>.

2. Sproul, RC. "The Covenant of Marriage: Truth That Can Transform Your Marriage." *The Covenant of Marriage.* 21 Feb. 2015. Web.<http://www.preceptaustin.org/the_covenant_of_marriage.htm>.

3. Hayford, Jack. "The Covenant of Marriage: Truth That Can Transform Your Marriage." *The Covenant of Marriage.* 21 Feb. 2015. Web. <http://www.preceptaustin.org/the_covenant_of_marriage.htm>.

4. Hurt, Bruce. "The Covenant of Marriage: Truth That Can Transform Your Marriage." *The Covenant of Marriage.* 21 Feb. 2015. Web. <http://www.preceptaustin.org/the_covenant_of_marriage.htm>.

5. Chapman, Gary D. "Contract Marriages." *Covenant Marriage: Building Communication & Intimacy.* Nashville: Broadman & Holman, 2003. 8-10. Print.

6. Chapman, Gary D. "Covenant Marriages." *Covenant Marriage: Building Communication & Intimacy.* Nashville: Broadman & Holman, 2003. 11-24. Print.

Session 6: Communicate or Your Marriage Will Disintegrate

1. Society for Neuroscience. "Language protein differs in males, females." *ScienceDaily.* ScienceDaily, 19 February 2013. <www.sciencedaily.com/releases/2013/02/130219172153.htm>.

2. Dr. Willard Harley, Jr. is our mentor in the area of making marriages fun and enjoyable and the best resource we have found. To completely master his approach to this issue, please visit: http://www.marriagebuilders.com. We also recommend adding his book, *His Needs, Her Needs,* to your marriage resource library. *His Needs, Her Needs* is designed to change the course of a marriage. Using a conversational style, Dr. Harley helps couples understand why their best intentions are not enough to prevent marital incompatibility. Couples must do more than want to meet each other's needs – they must actually meet them!

3. Evans, Jimmy, and Karen Evans. "The Secrets of Successful Communication." *Marriage Today*. YouTube. Web. <www.MarriageToday.tv>.

4. Smalley, Michael and Amy Smalley. "The Satisfied Marriage Training Manual for Christians." Woodlands: Smalley Impact, LLC. 2008.

5. Chapman, Gary D. "Covenant Marriages." *5 Love Languages*. Chicago: Northfield Publishing. 1992. www.5lovelanguages.com.

Session 7: Caring Enough to Embrace Conflict

1. Sollee, Diane. The Coalition for Marriage, Family and Couples Education, LLC., 2015. Web. <http://www.smartmarriages.com/divorcepredictor.html>

2. Anonymous. "Two Natures Beat Within My Chest." <http://www.spiritandtruth.org/teaching/Book_of_1st_Corinthians/06_1Cor_3_1-4/1Cor_3_1-4_Notes.htm>

Session 8: Roles and Responsibilities: Being a Godly Husband and a Godly Wife

1. Hendriksen, William, and Simon Kistemaker. "Ephesians." *New Testament Commentary*. Grand Rapids: Baker Book House, 1953. Print.

2. Rainey, Dennis. "What Should Be the Husband's Role in Marriage." *Family Life*. 2002. Web. <http://www.familylife.com/articles/topics/marriage/staying-married/husbands/what-should-be-the-husbands-role-in-marriage#.VQ22IcYID0Q>.

3. Murphy, Deborah. "Marriage Teaching – Biblical Roles of Men & Women." *Marriage Teaching – Biblical Roles of Men & Women*. Maranatha Life, 2001. Web. <http://maranathalife.com/marriage/mar-rel5.htm>.

Session 9: The Money

1. The entire chapter was co-authored by Talaat and Tai of www.hisandhermoney.com.

2. "Ron Blue's Simple Message of Stewardship | Stewardship Central." *Stewardship Central.* Lampo Licensing, LLC. Web. <http://www.stewardshipcentral.org/posts/ron-blues-simple-message-of-stewardship>.

Session 10: Sanctified, Satisfying, and Sizzling Married Sex!

1. Slattery, Dr. Juli. *Authentic Intimacy.* Authentic Intimacy. Web. <http://authenticintimacy.com>. Blog. Juli Slattery is a widely known clinical psychologist, author, speaker, and broadcast media professional. She co-founded Authentic Intimacy (www.authenticintimacy.com) and is the co-author of several books including Passion Pursuit: What Kind of Love Are You Making and Pulling Back The Shades – http://www.pullingbacktheshades.com/

2. Clinebell, Howard John, and Charlotte H. Clinebell. "Chapter 2: The Many Facets of Intimacy." *The Intimate Marriage.* New York: Harper & Row, 1970. Print.

Session 11: Prepared Parents

1. Barna, George. *Transforming Children into Spiritual Champions.* Ventura, Calif.: Regal, 2003. Print.

2. McDowell, Josh. "7 A's – Building Relationships." *Josh.org*. Josh McDowell Ministry, 23 July 2012. Web. <http://www.josh.org/video-2/building-relationships/>.

3. Fields, Doug. "Disciplining Positively." *Purpose-driven Youth Ministry: 9 Essential Foundations for Healthy Growth.* Grand Rapids, Mich.: Zondervan, 1998. 328. Print.

4. Ursinus, Zacharias. *The Commentary of Dr. Zacharias Ursinus on the Heidelberg Catechism.* Phillipsburg, NJ: Presbyterian and Reformed Pub., 1985. 65-66. Print.

5. Ursinus, Zacharias. *The Commentary of Dr. Zacharias Ursinus on the Heidelberg Catechism.* Phillipsburg, NJ: Presbyterian and Reformed Pub., 1985. Print.

Notes

Session 12: Blended/Bonded Family: "We Do...Again"

1. This entire chapter was co-authored by Rev. Dr. Bobby L. Love and his wife, Janice R. Love.

2. "Stepfamily Statistics." *The Stepfamily Foundation Inc.* Web. <http://www.stepfamily.org/stepfamily-statistics.html>.

Session 13: Are You Sure You Want to Do This?

1. Blackaby, Henry T., and Melvin Blackaby. *Experiencing God Together: God's Plan to Touch Your World.* Nashville: Broadman & Holman, 2002. Print.

Testimonials

I can honestly say the Lord God Almighty in His divine wisdom and knowledge knew exactly what I needed when he allowed me to meet Jim and Teresa Adams. I don't know and I don't want to even think about where I would be in my marriage if it wasn't for the information and guidance that I have received through their counsel and care.

I strongly recommend any who is interested in Biblical based instruction for marriage and family to seek them out but only if you are interested in the truth of God's plan is for a husband, wife, and family unit.

I am still happily married today and I owe and large part of that to the rich in depth counseling from Jim and Teresa Adams.

Charlie J. – Jackson, MS

Whether entertaining me on long drives to visit family, or enlightening me during leisurely strolls in my neighborhood , listening to the podcasts, has become one of my most rewarding past times. Jim and Teresa's wisdom and expertise on marriage and family relationship topics shared on the podcasts have motivated me to make relational adjustments in my life, and they have led me to a greater understanding of God's marital design.

I would have to say that the greatest evolution of attitudinal change has come in the area of finances in my marital relationship. The three part podcast series on finances (Money, Money, Money) was compellingly convincing and convicting. It was quite apparent that Jim and Teresa had done their research and were well knowledgeable on God's plan for using financial circumstances in our lives.

Through pointing out that how we handle money reflects our faith in God, the podcasts challenged me to surrender control and fully share in financial decision making with my husband. Knowing that financial matters are a leading contributor of divorce, I would rate these money – focused podcasts among the most important. This is my testimonial of the ability of Jim and Teresa to change marriages through compelling content via their well devised and professional delivery.

Dr. Evelyn Walker M.D. – Madison, MS

My now husband, Jerome, and I are really in your debt for all of the wonderful things that your ministries have done for us (I am speaking of premarital counseling, IronMen, and mentorship).

We not only began considering marriage and preparing for marriage under your mentorship, but this mentoring relationship also made us contemplate God calling us to get married sooner rather than later.

Soon after we met with you as a couple, you began to ask us about our future plans for marriage. I will never forget Jim saying, "Yeah, yeah, that's great and all, but help me understand why you are waiting to get married?" We truly didn't know, and here we are, about a year and a half and a lot of prayers later, married.

Through IronMen, I have seen Jerome grow from being a man with a girlfriend into a responsible, loving, caring, intentional, and understanding husband.

I know that God has been using you and your ministry to cultivate that within him. Also, going to premarital counseling was one of the best things that we could have done for our relationship. We were brought face to face with the extreme (and sometimes unrealistic) expectations we had for each other and overcame the conflicts that came along with them because of the skills that we learned in premarital counseling.

We have learned to communicate effectively in loving ways and find out what's right, not who's right in every situation.

Our married life is now blossoming all because our fellowships, our premarital counseling, and our mentoring are all based on a solid foundation, the Word of God.

Thank you so much Jim and Teresa,
from Jerome and Analise – Jackson, MS

Thank you both so much for this tremendous resource I'm excited to be a part. Teresa I'm coming to MS and would love to have tea or just chat. So much has happened since you helped me find my way again. And the journey has been beyond amazing.

K. Ridley – Omaha, NE

We met Jim and Teresa through friends that attend their church. They asked us if we were planning on having martial counseling before getting married. We had not given it much thought

Jim and Teresa explained in depth God's Plan, The Expectations, and The Joys of Marriage.
They have created an entire counseling program based on what God says and they outlined the purposes of marriage.

We learned so much in that time. Our relationship grew with each other and more importantly our individual relationships with God.

It was so beautiful reading together and praying together and understanding the Lord and who he is. There were many lessons that were taught, however, the one that my husband and I hold fast to the most is in this marriage we are to try and "out-please" the other.

This program has blessed us immensely on understanding so much that is to come in our marriage. God blessed us with this gift of a person to spend the rest of our life with and we need to know the best way to do that.

Thank You,
Jeremy and Kendra Courtney – Jackson, MS

Truly amazing material! You guys are adorable.

Charles A – Memphis, TN

Jim and Teresa get right to the point on major relationship issues.

Mike T – Lexington, KY

Jim and Teresa clearly know what they are talking about. Great resource. Their passion and knowledge jumps off the pages

Nick P. – Boston, MA

In a society where divorce has become so prevalent, this is the kind of resource that everyone need. Today it seems like married couples are ready to run to the divorce lawyers at the first sign of disagreement and this tool is all about getting couples to work through issues and stay together.

Hector A – Austin, TX

Jim and Teresa have created a tremendous resource- full of honesty, authenticity, and transparency about the ups and downs life throws at you and how to journey together as a unified couple. Fabulous resource no matter your current relationship status.

M. Mitchell – Memphis, TN

Made in the USA
Charleston, SC
11 June 2015